Spring Coloring Book

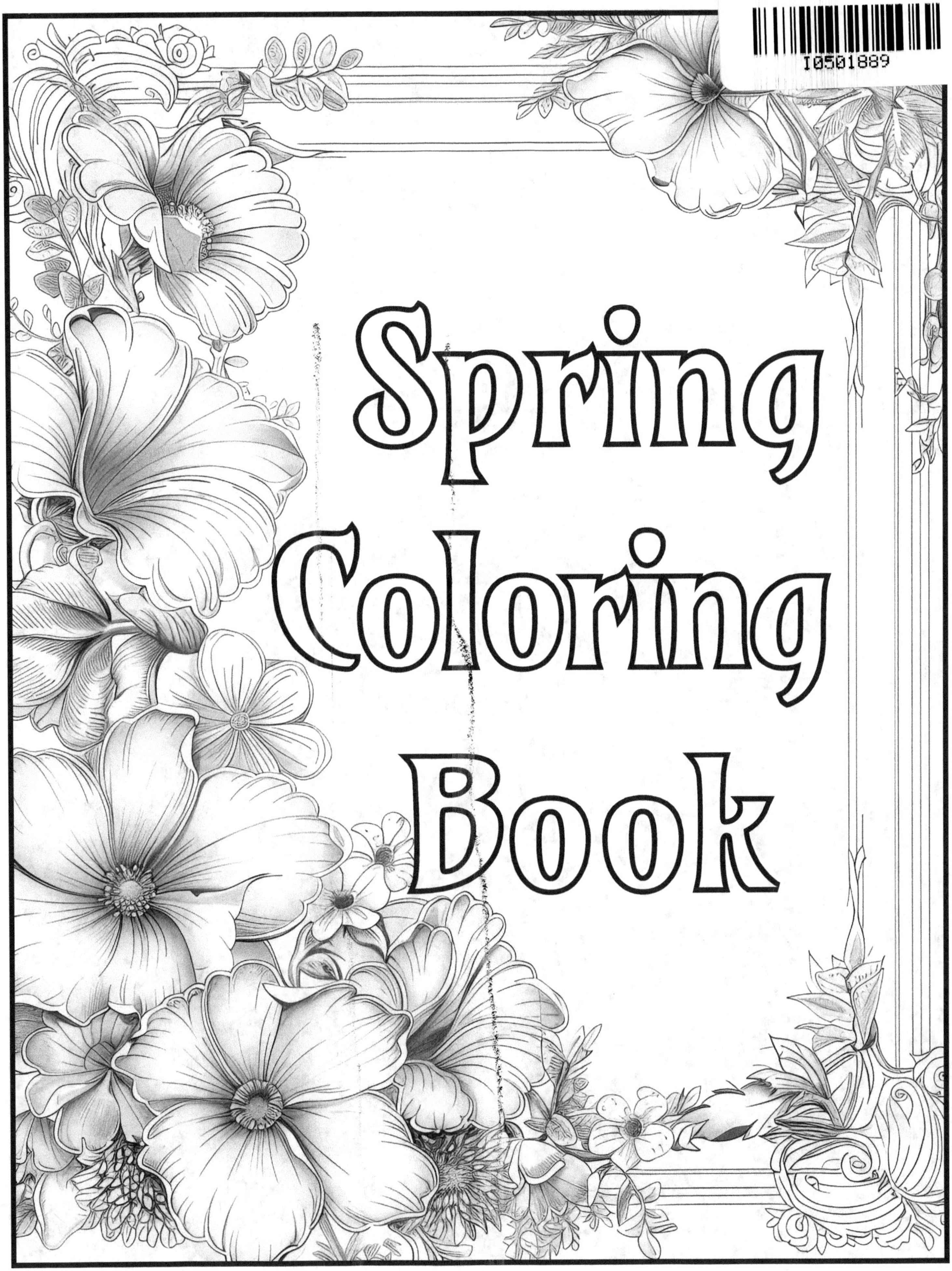

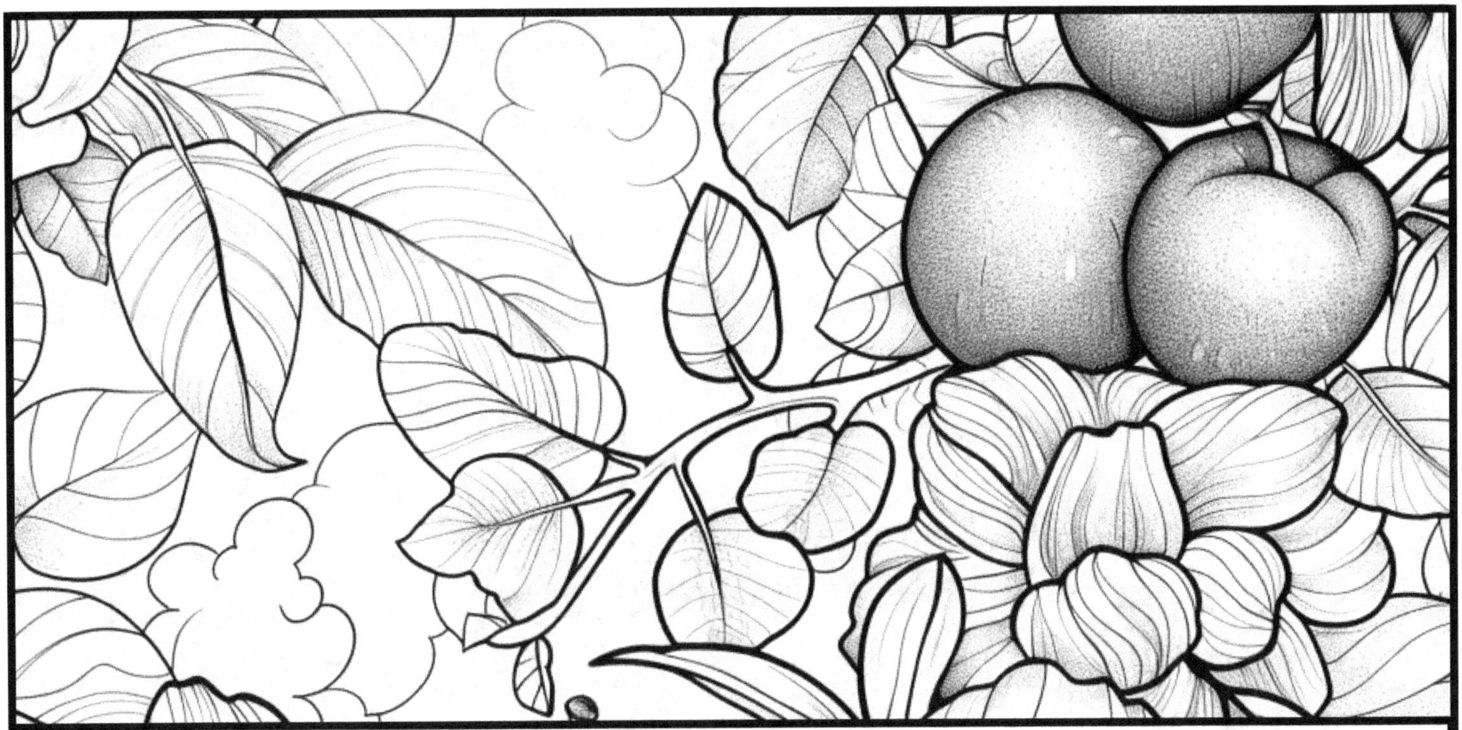

This book belongs to:

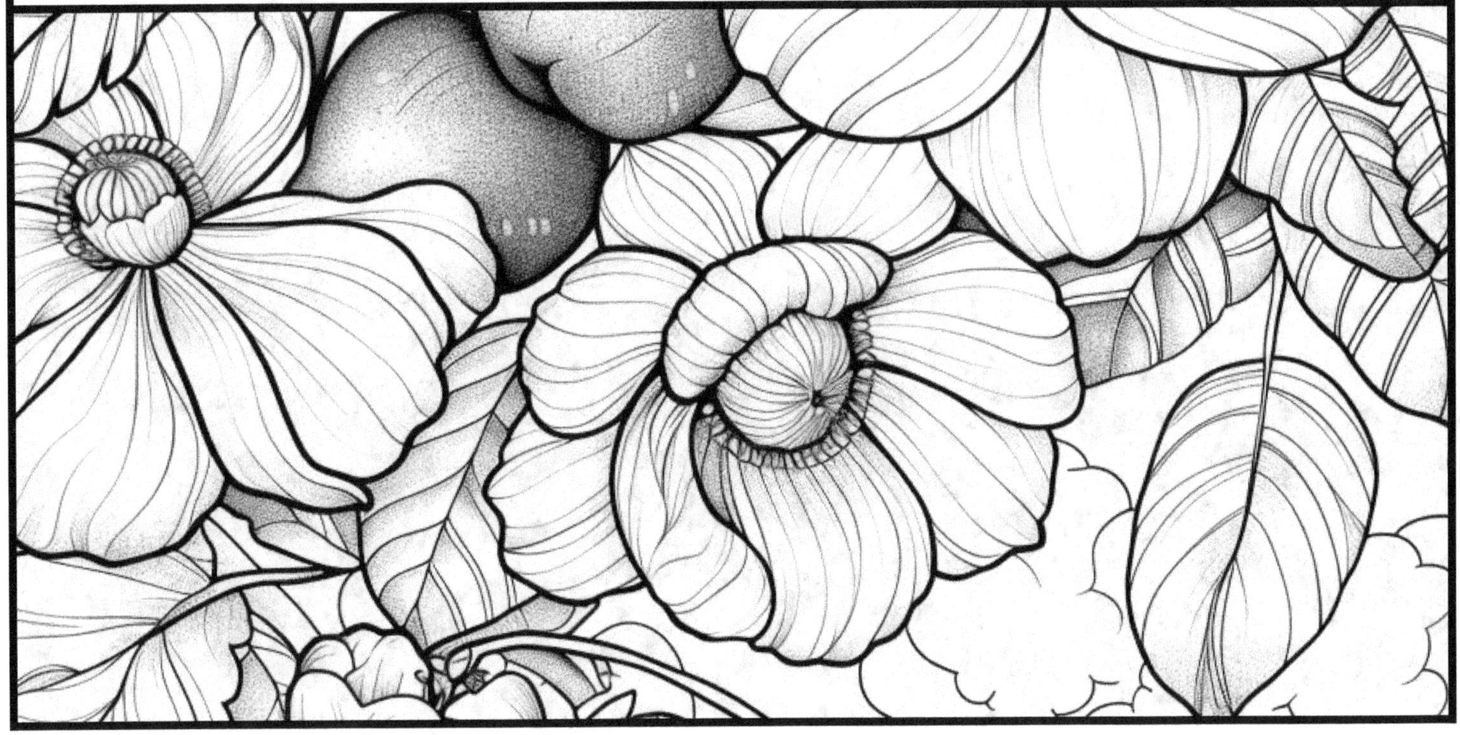

Color Test Page

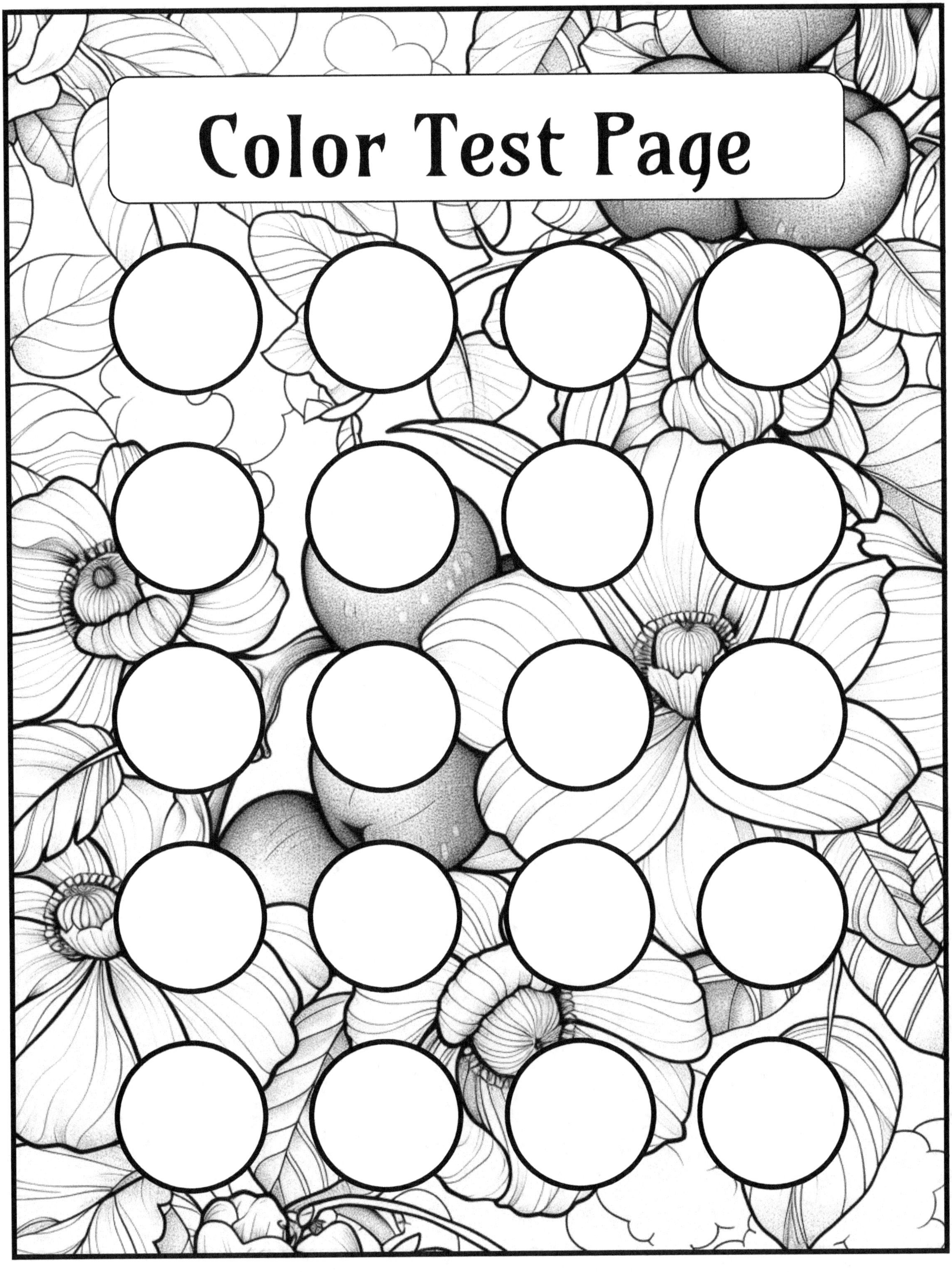

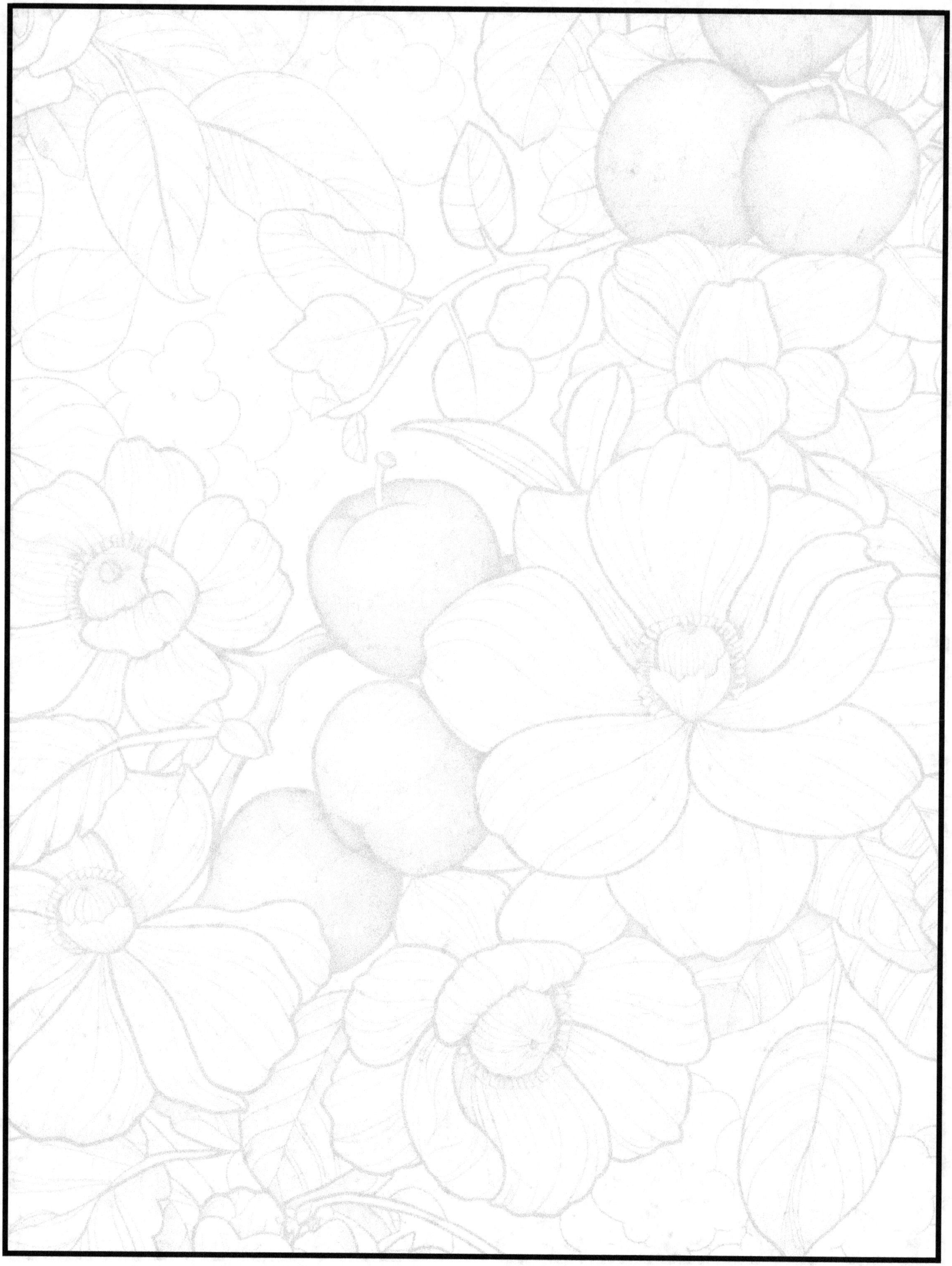

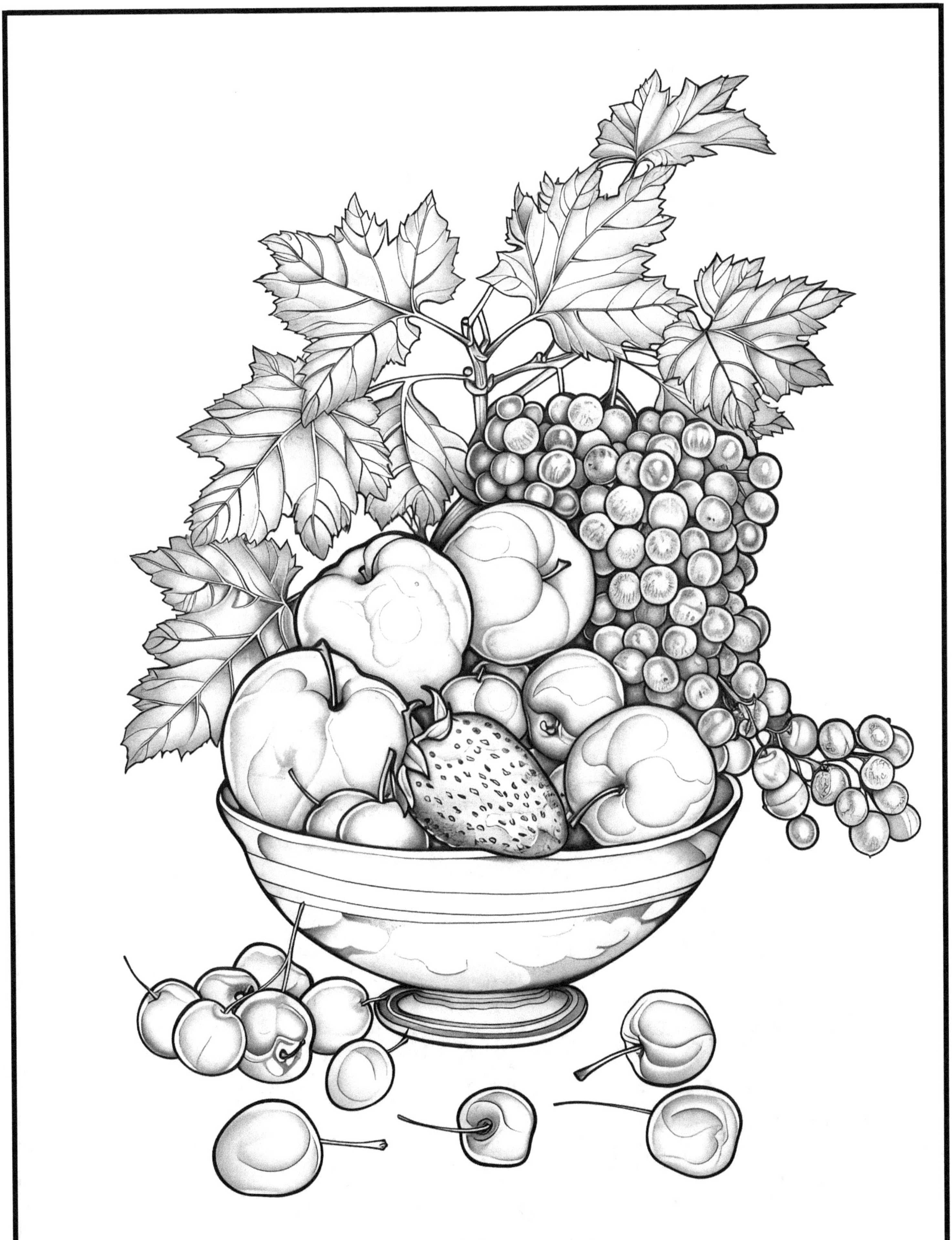

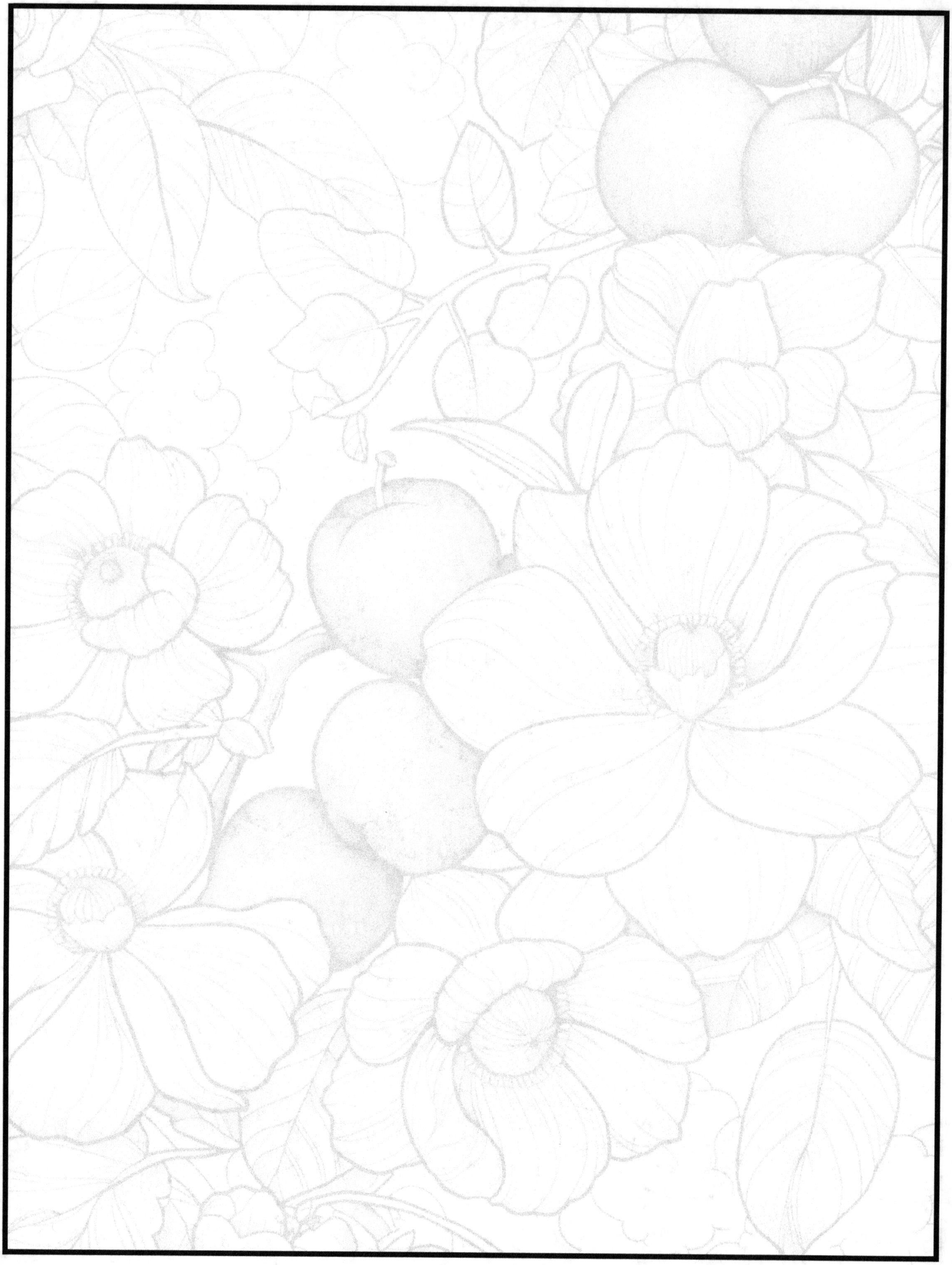

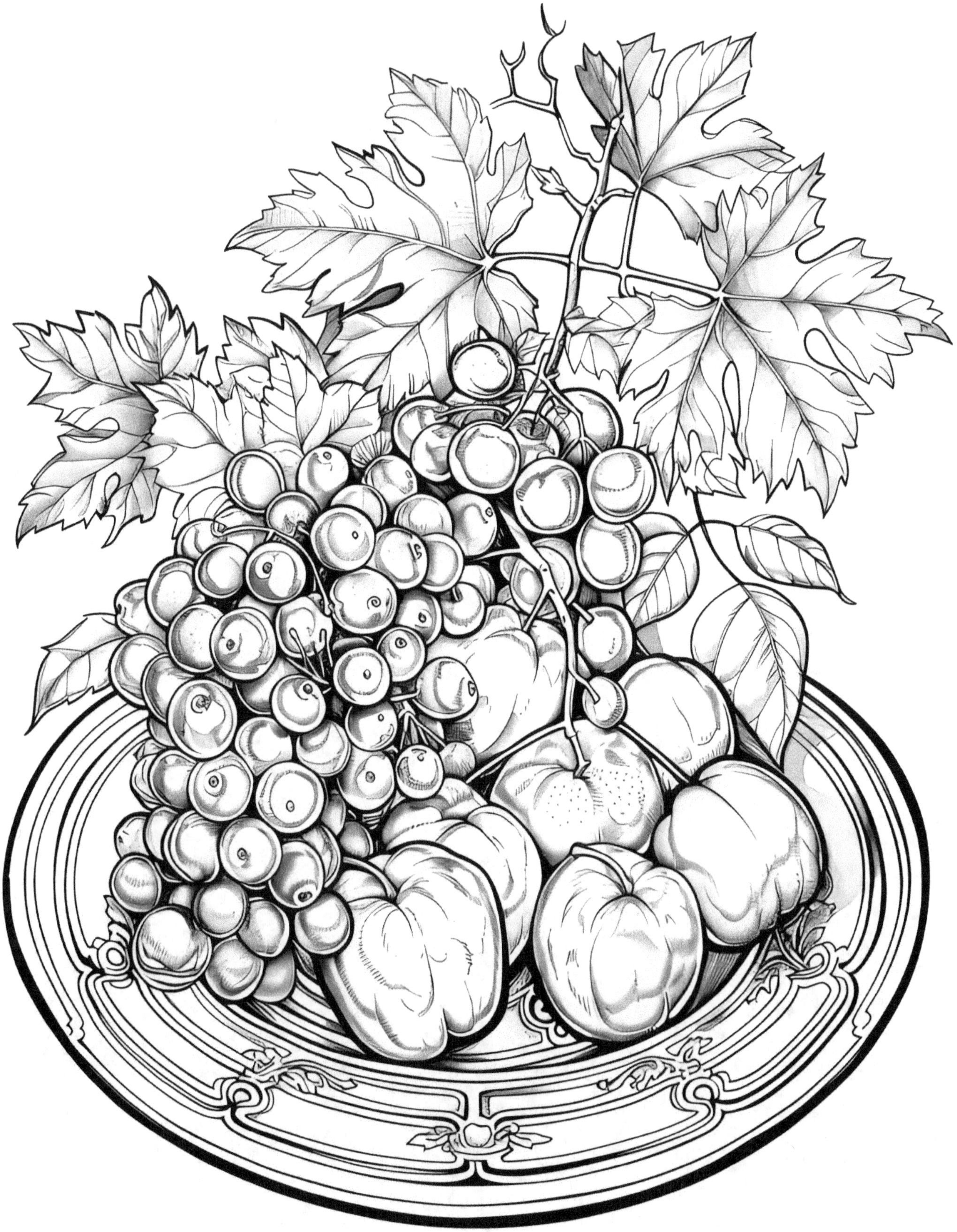

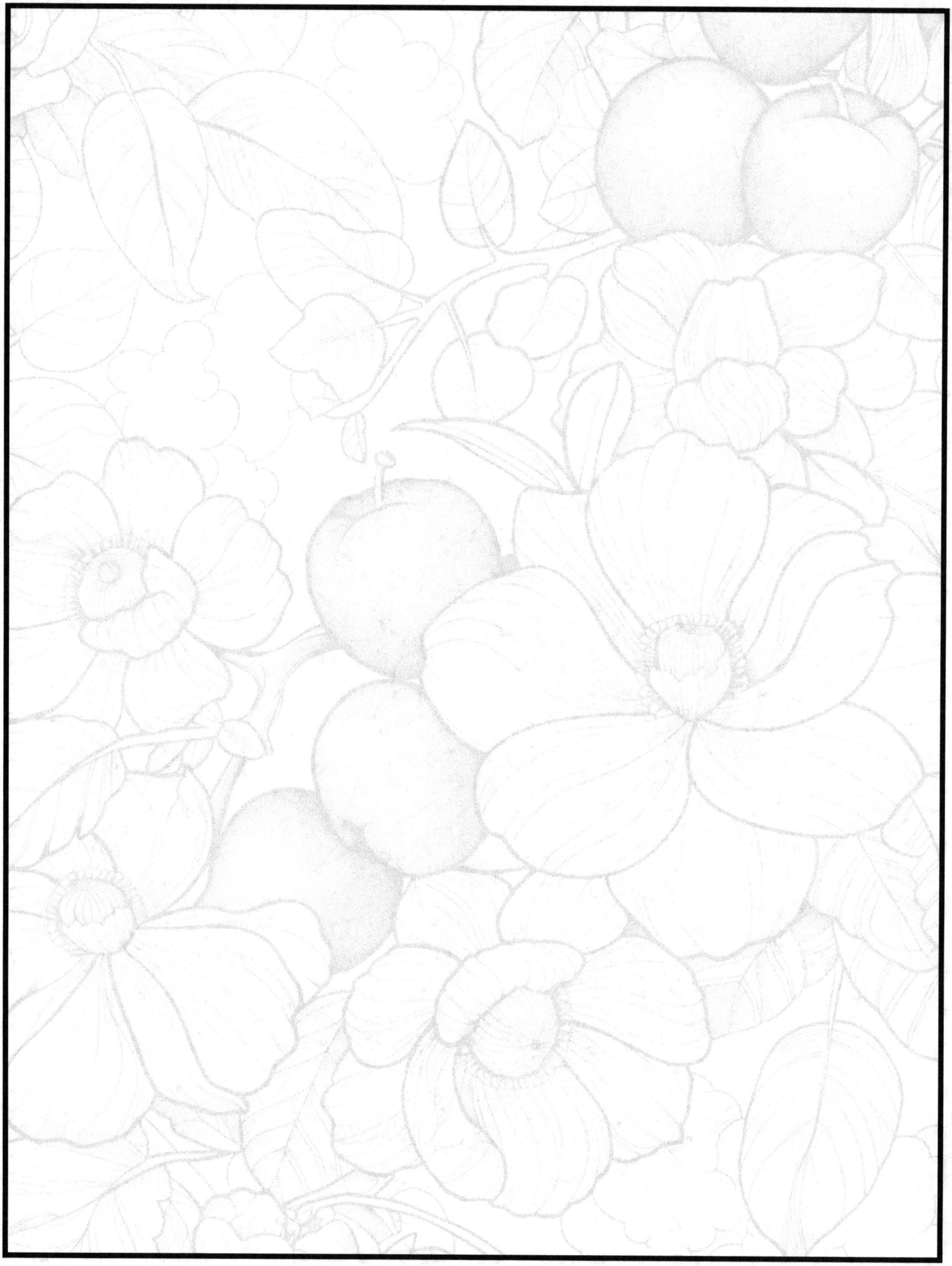

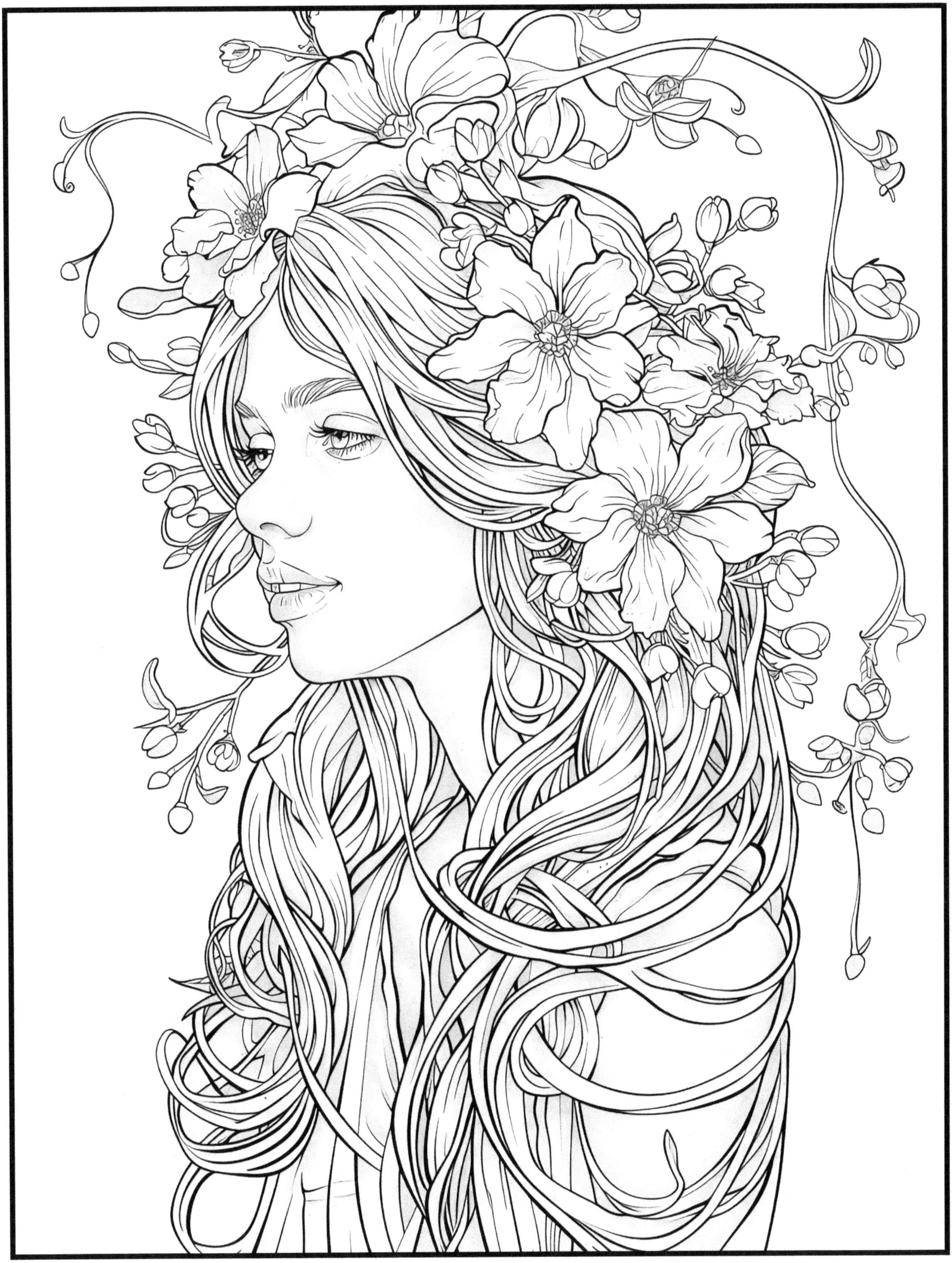

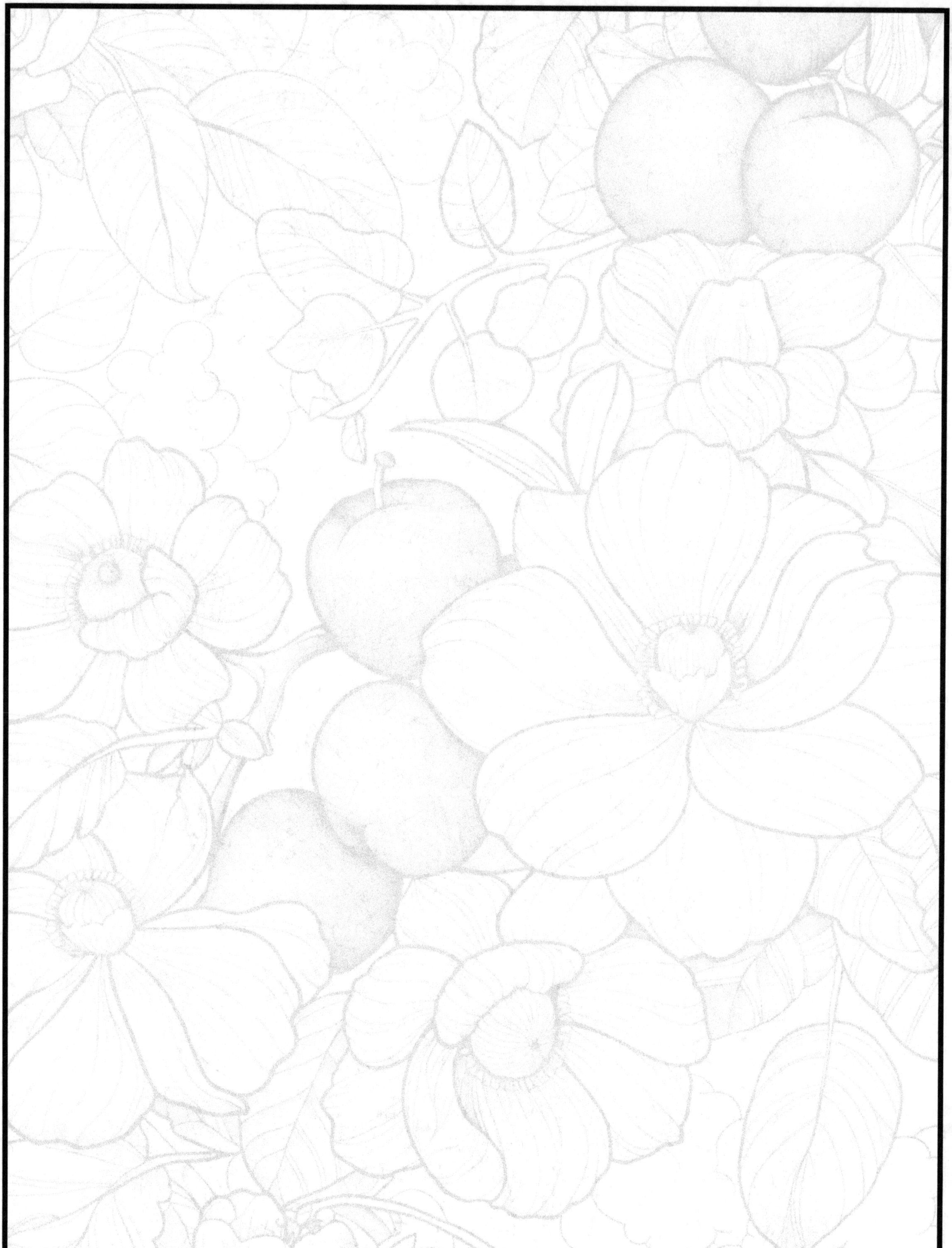

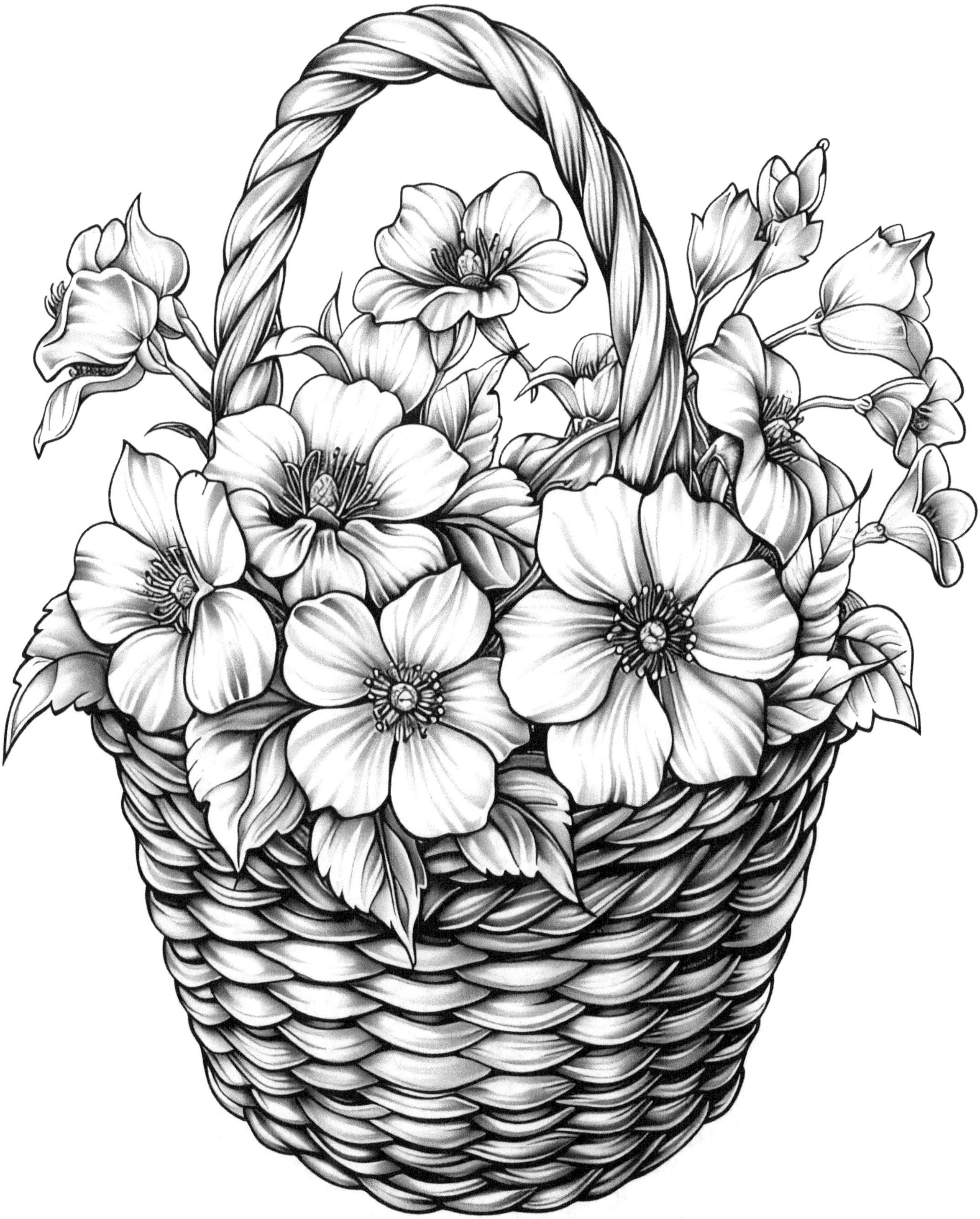

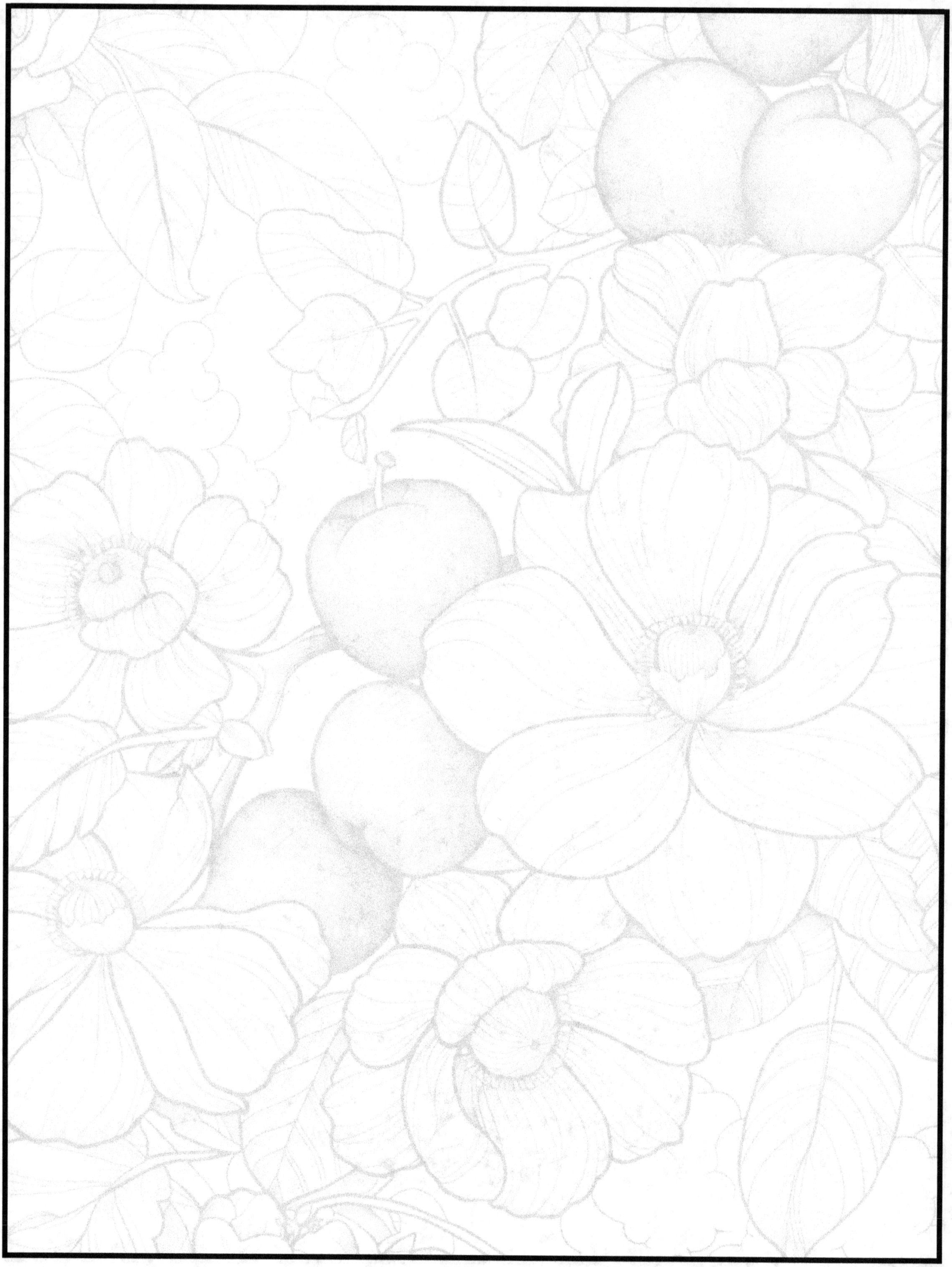

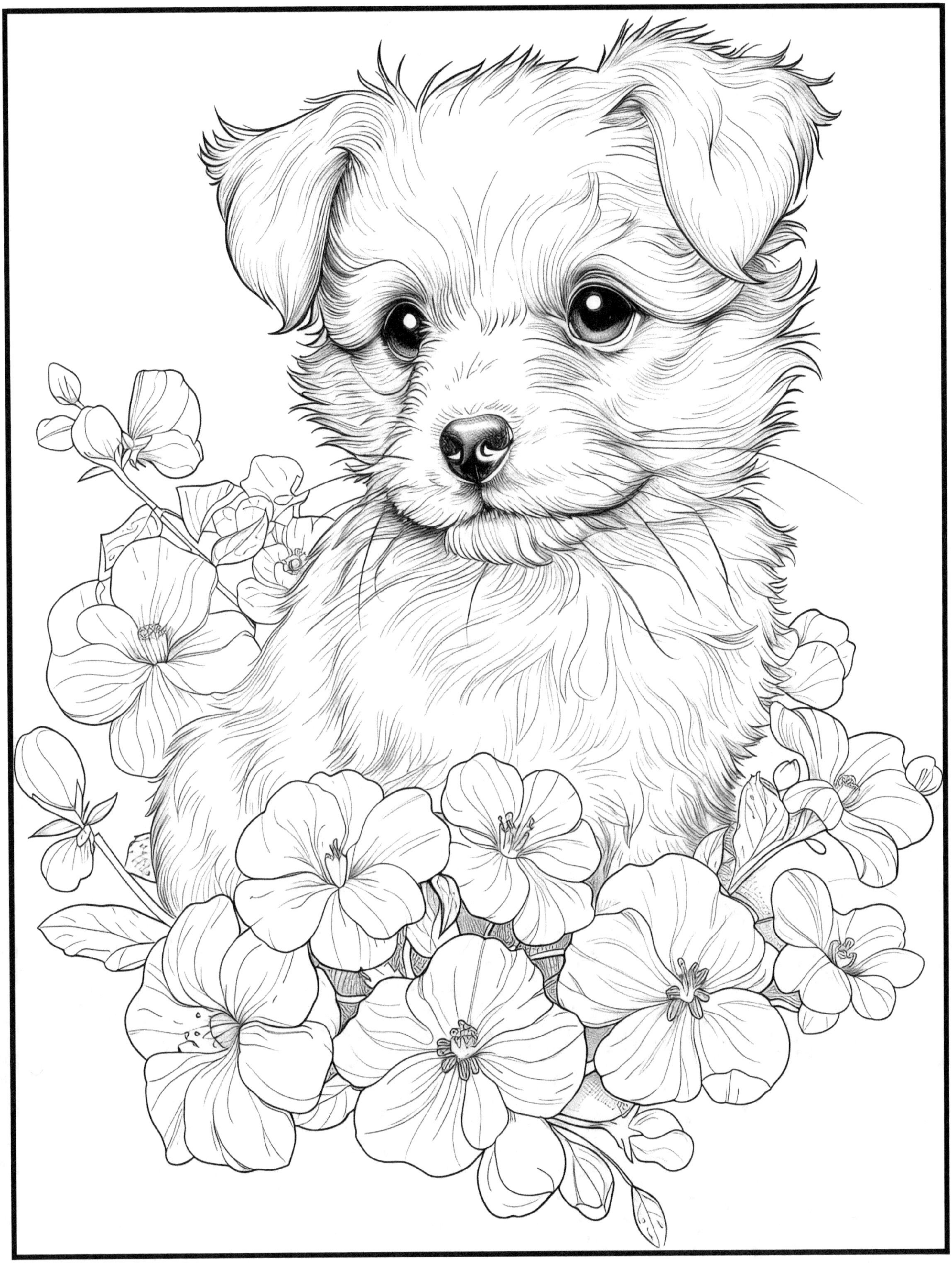

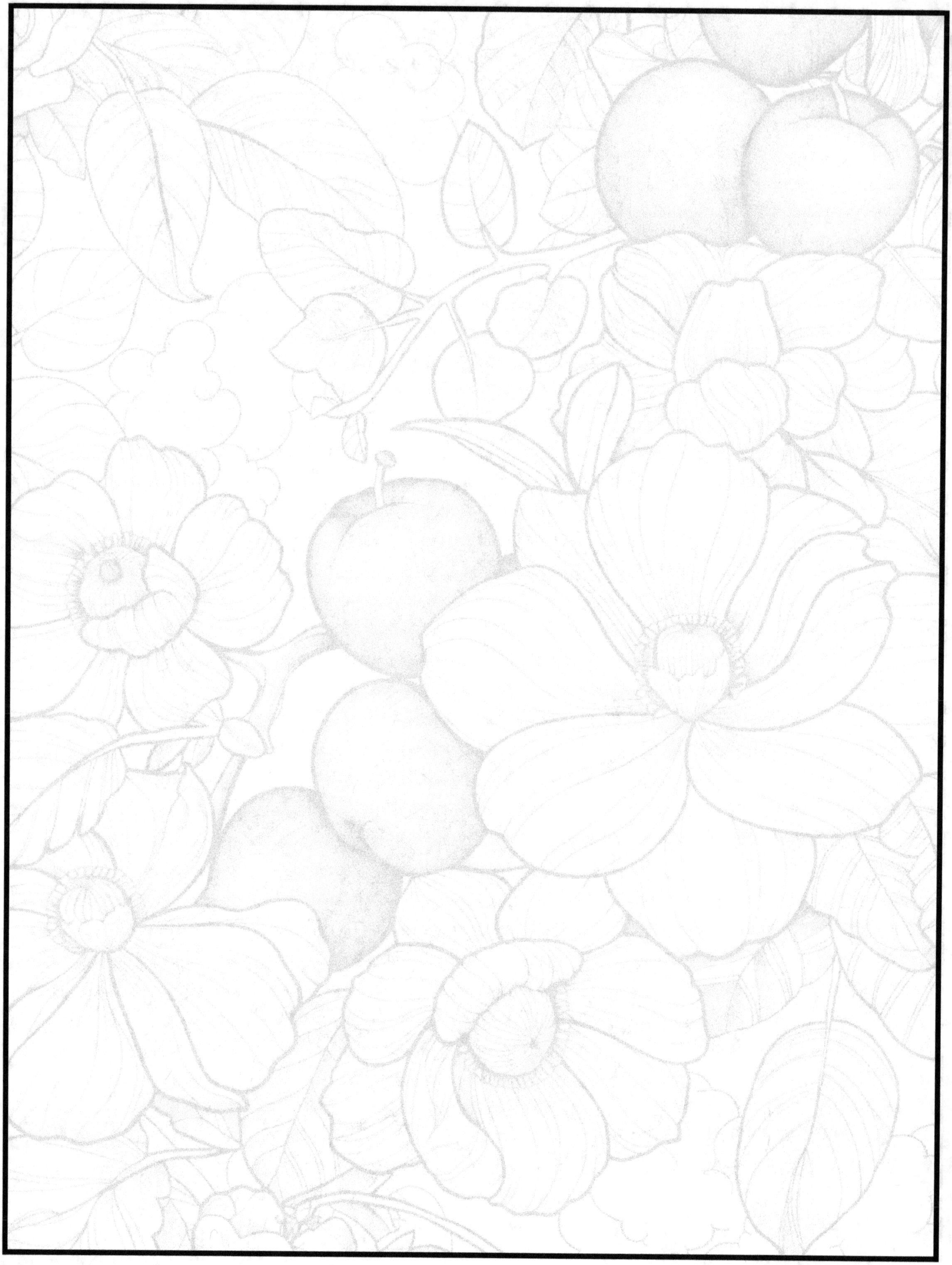

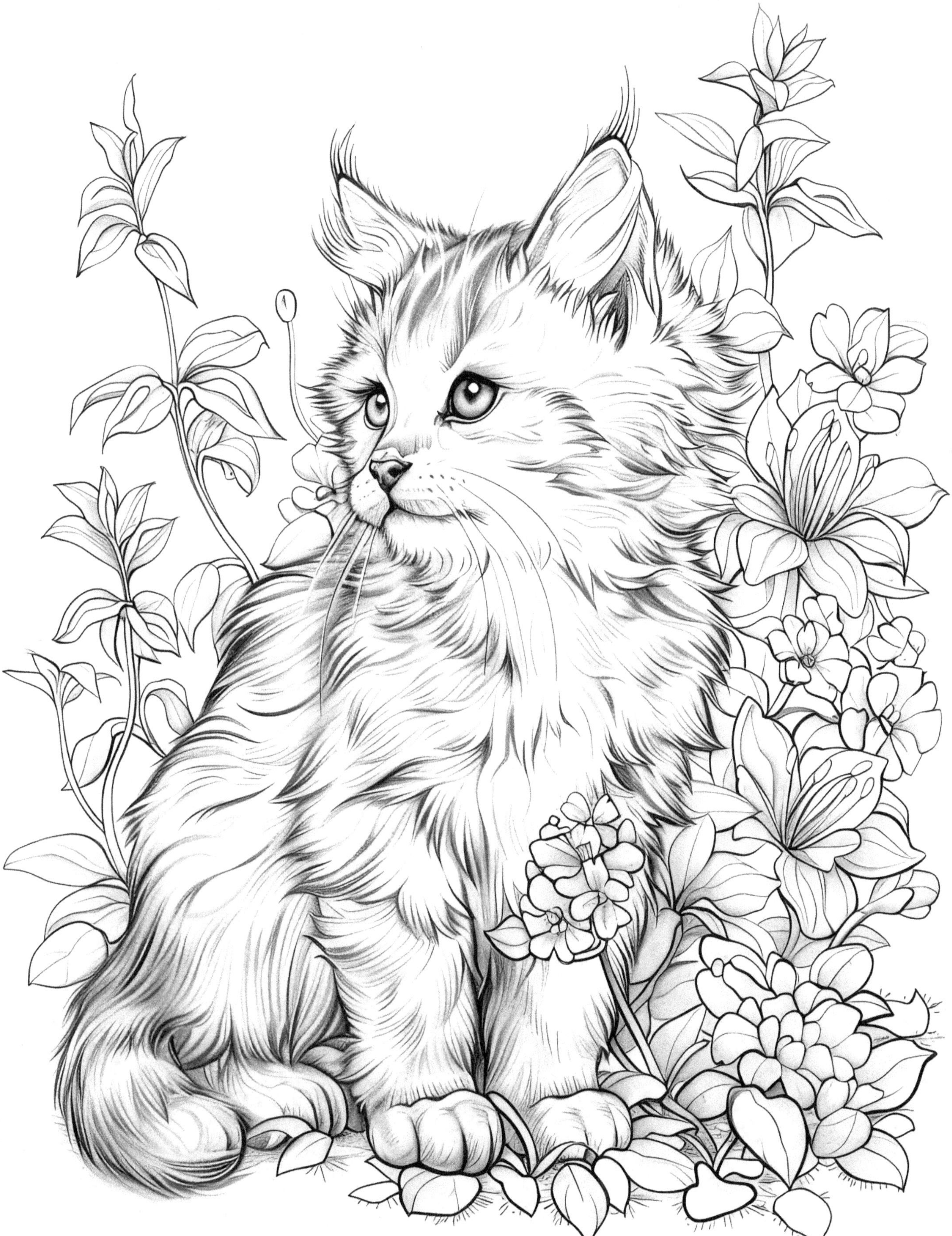

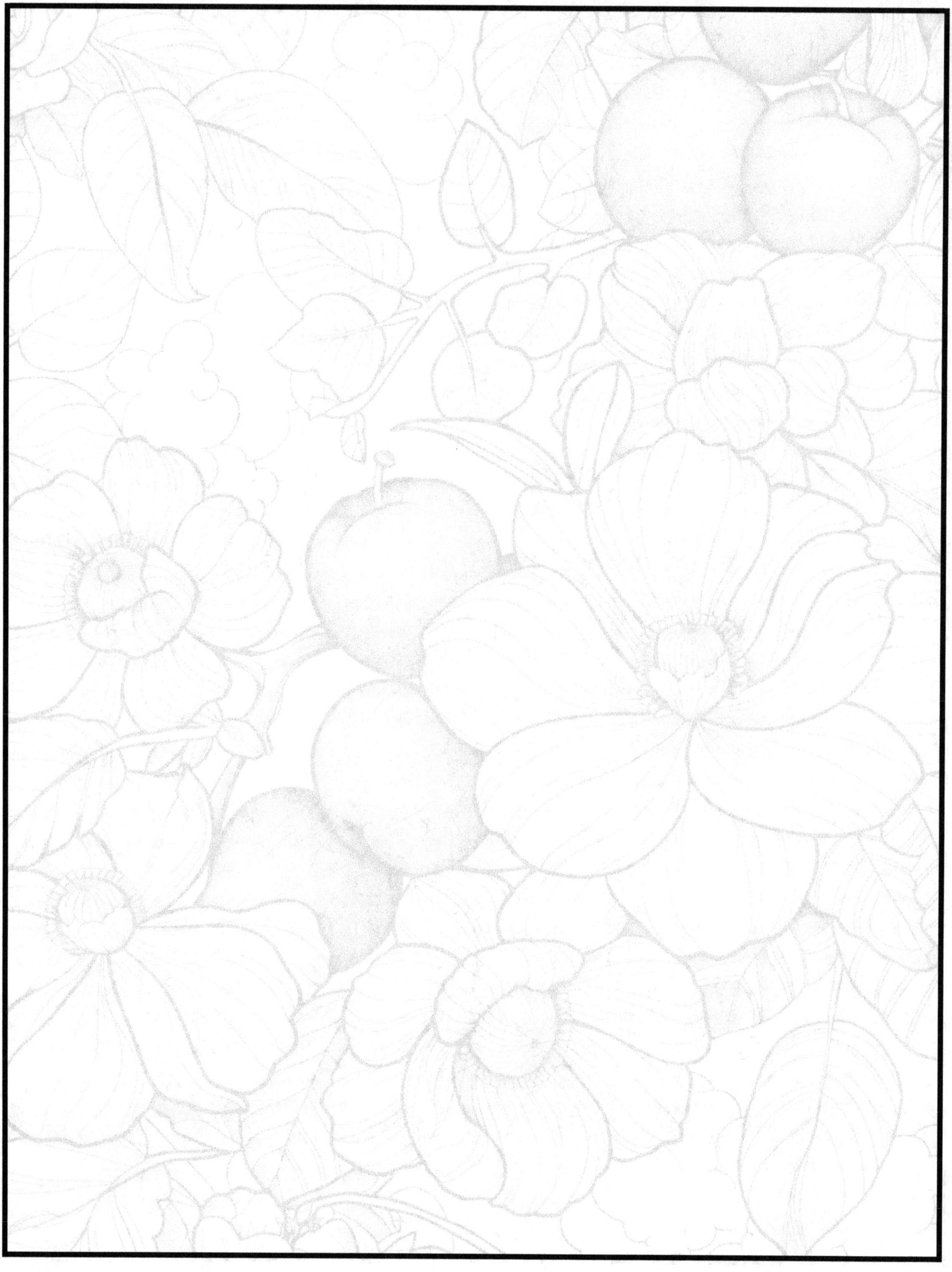

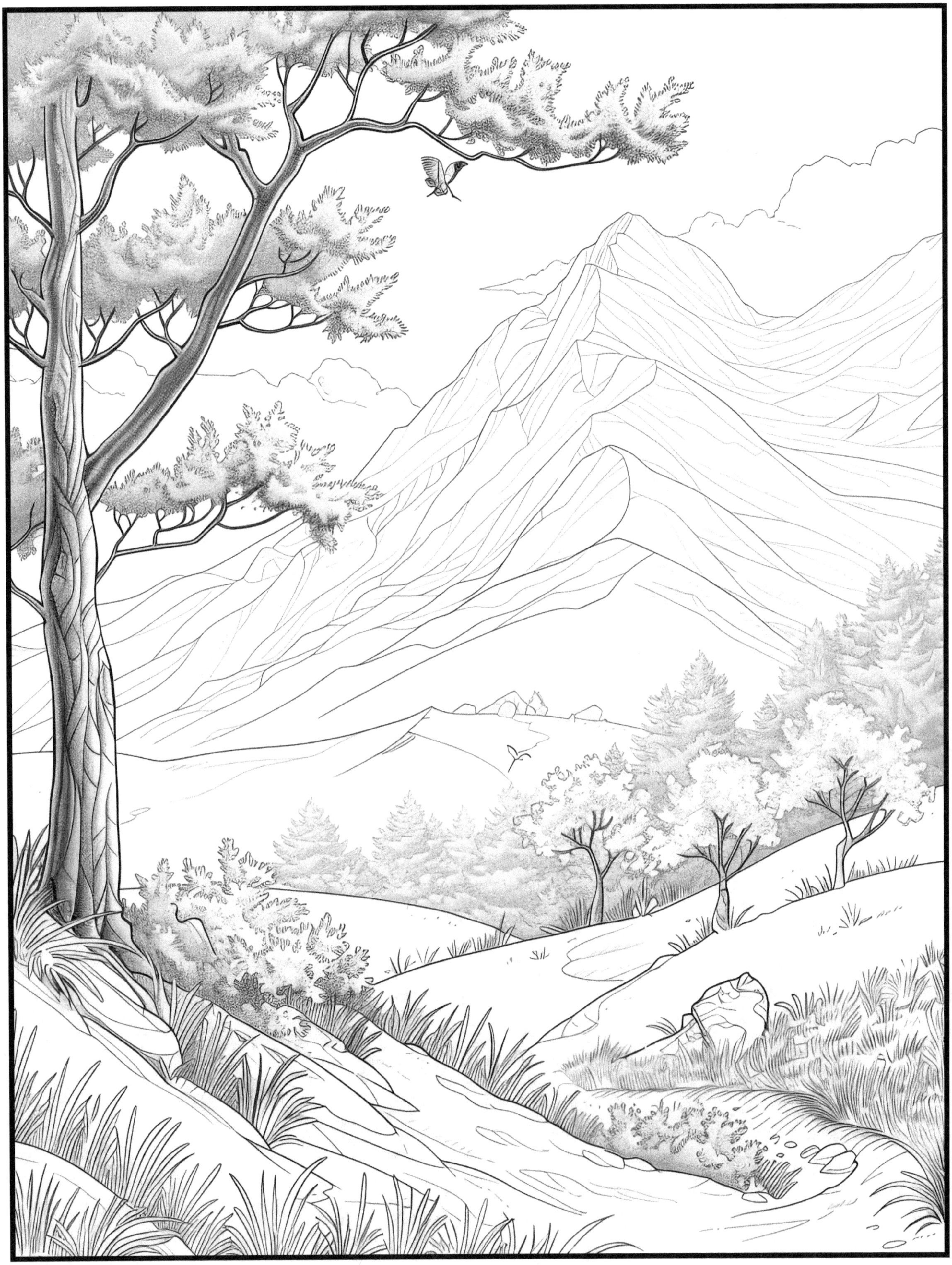

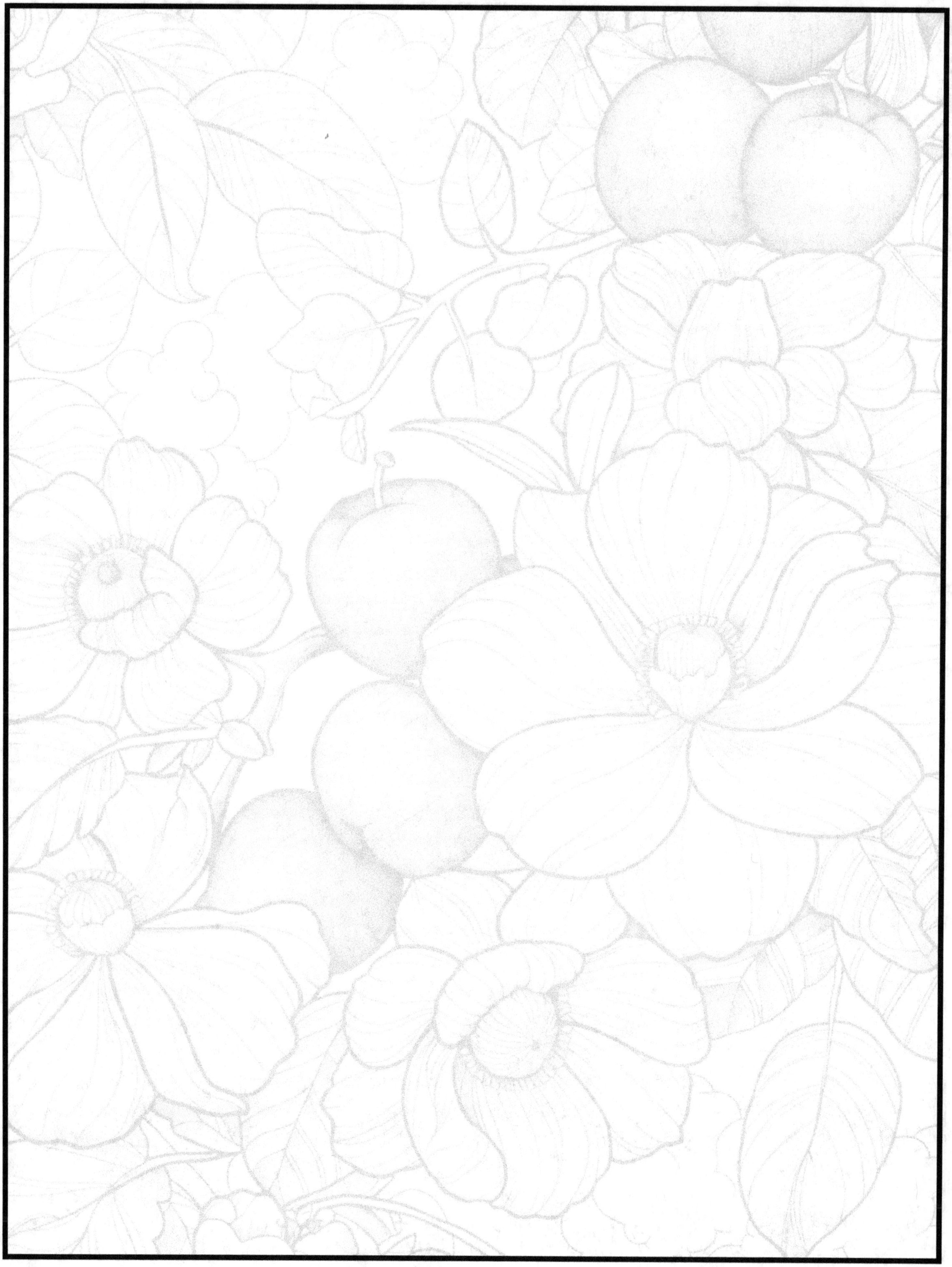

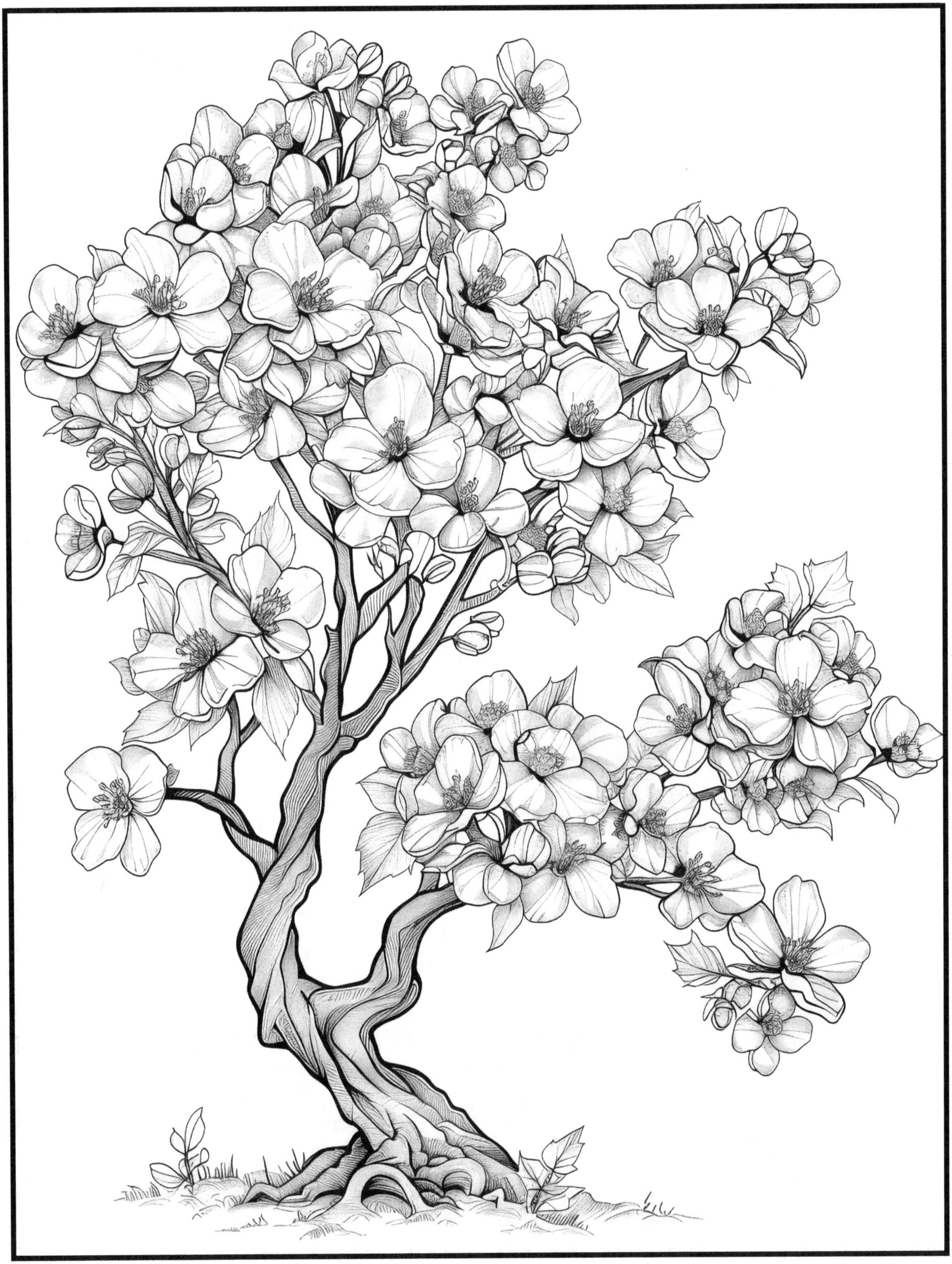

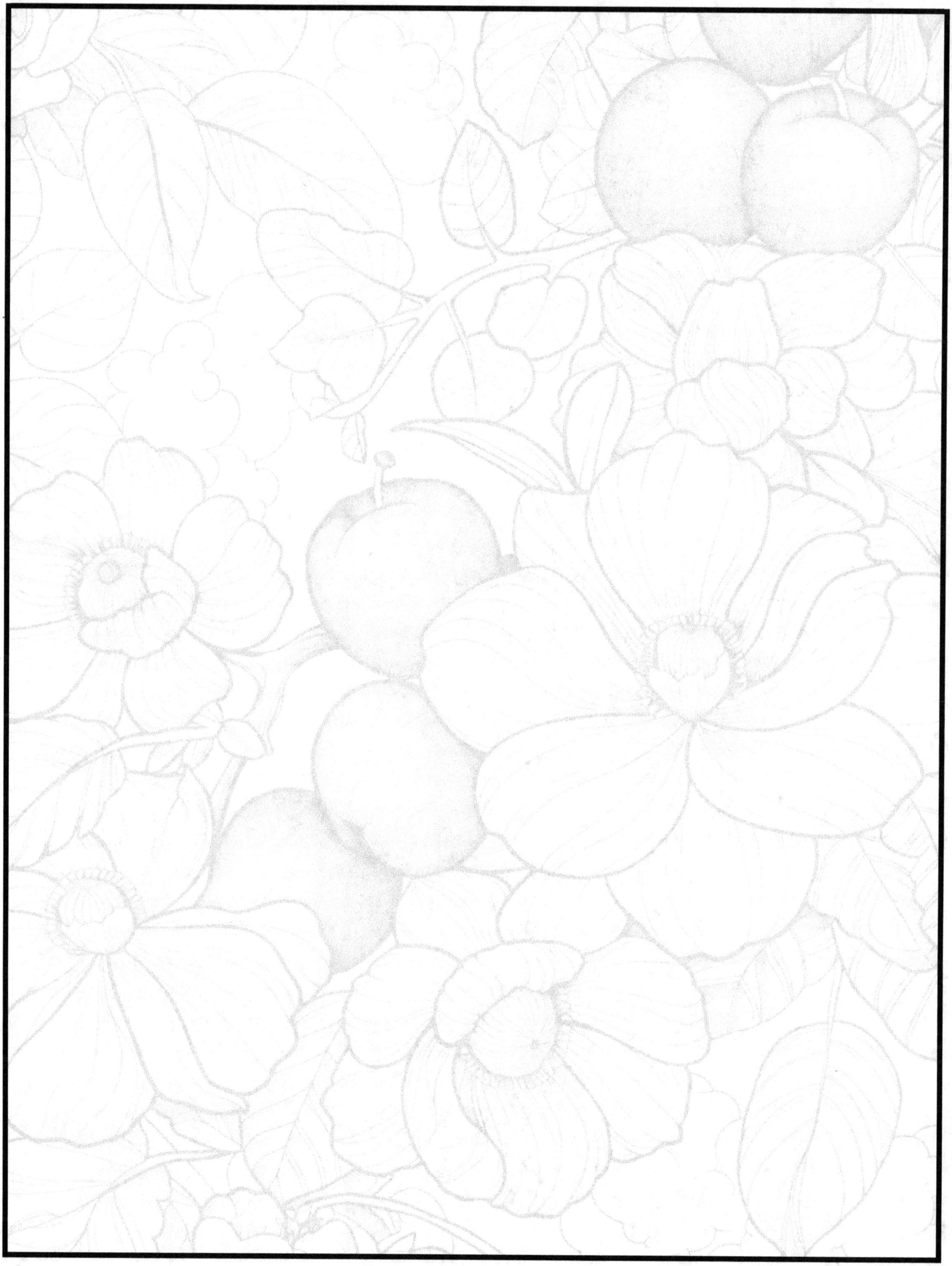

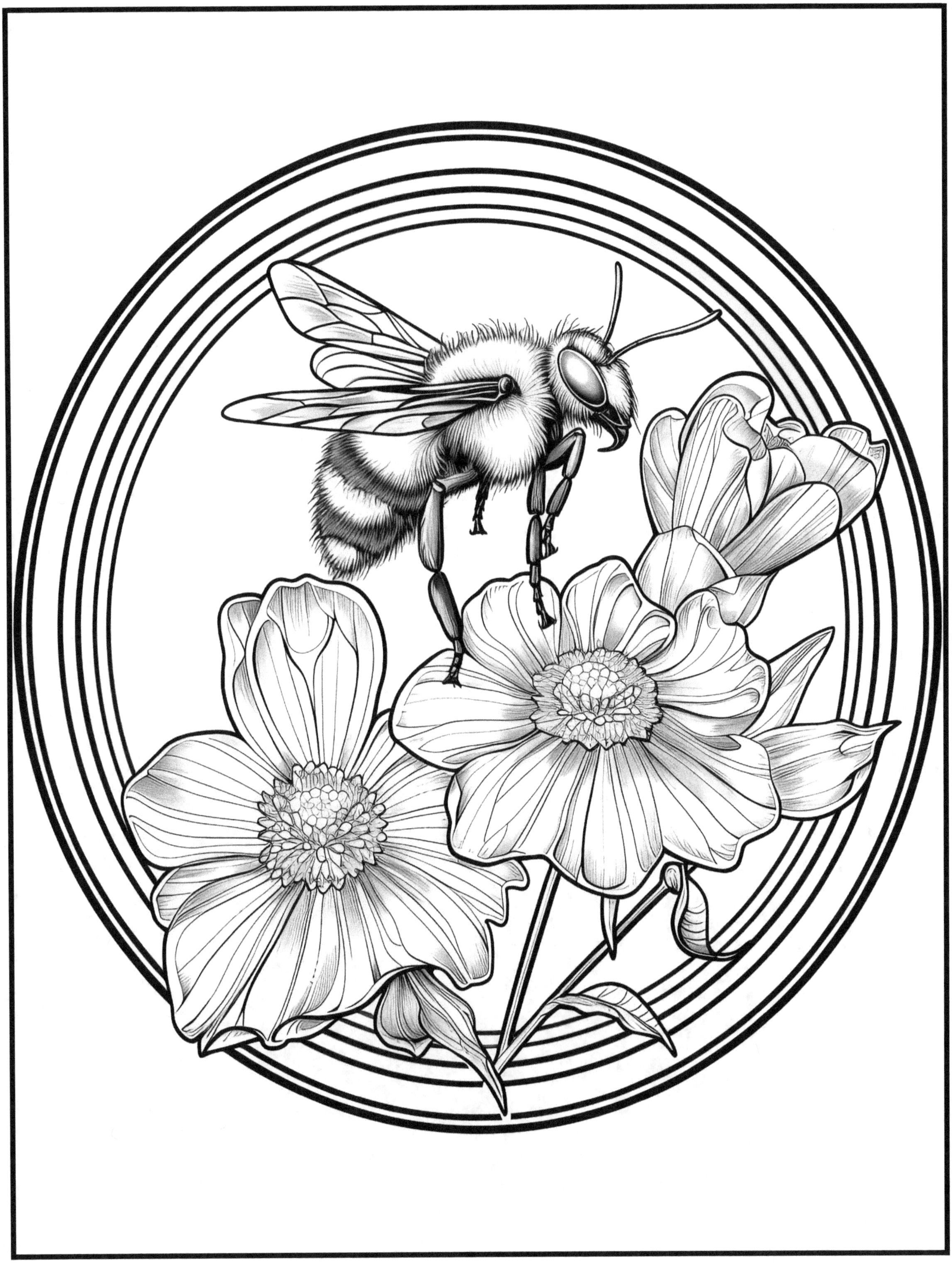

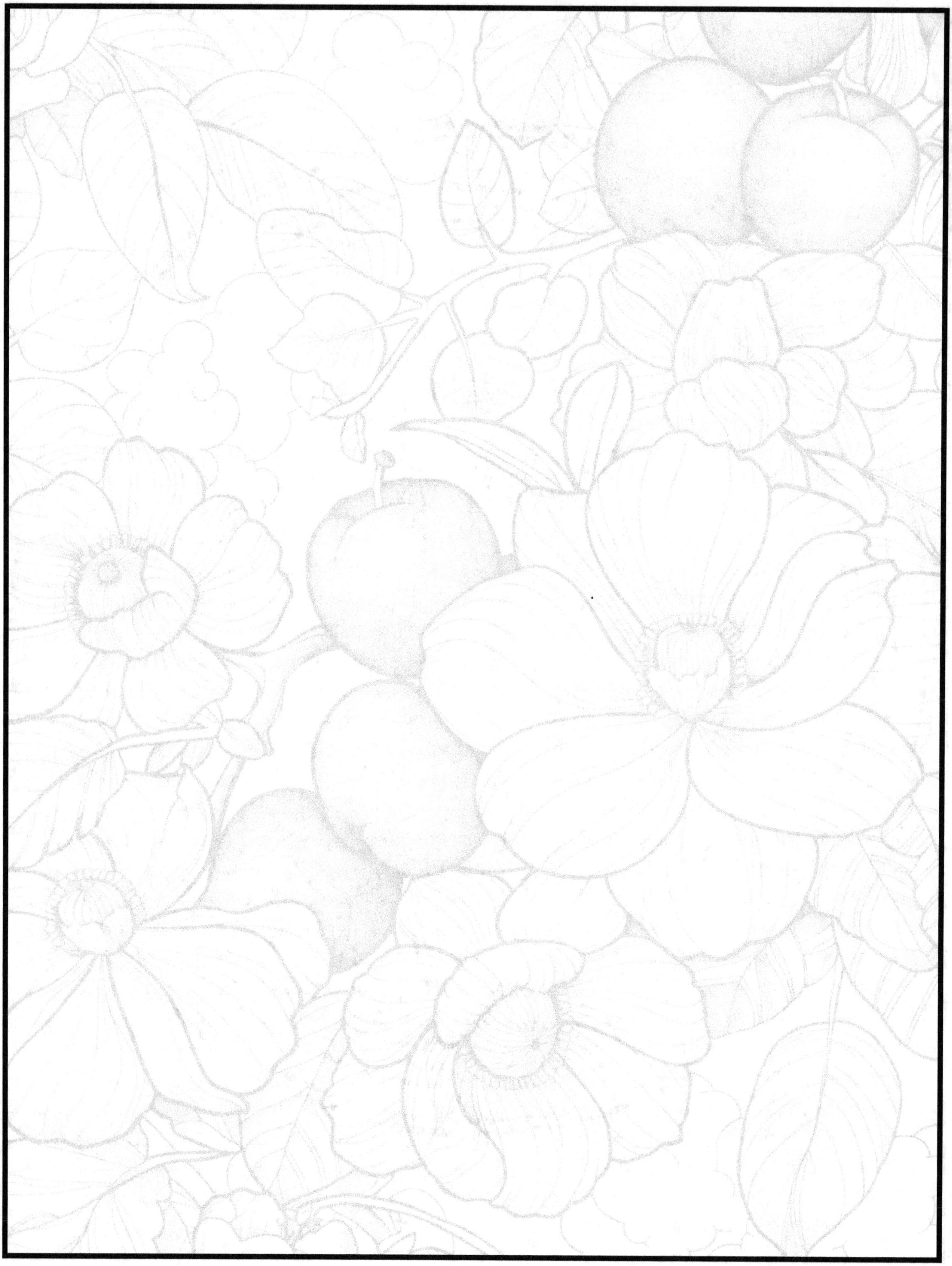

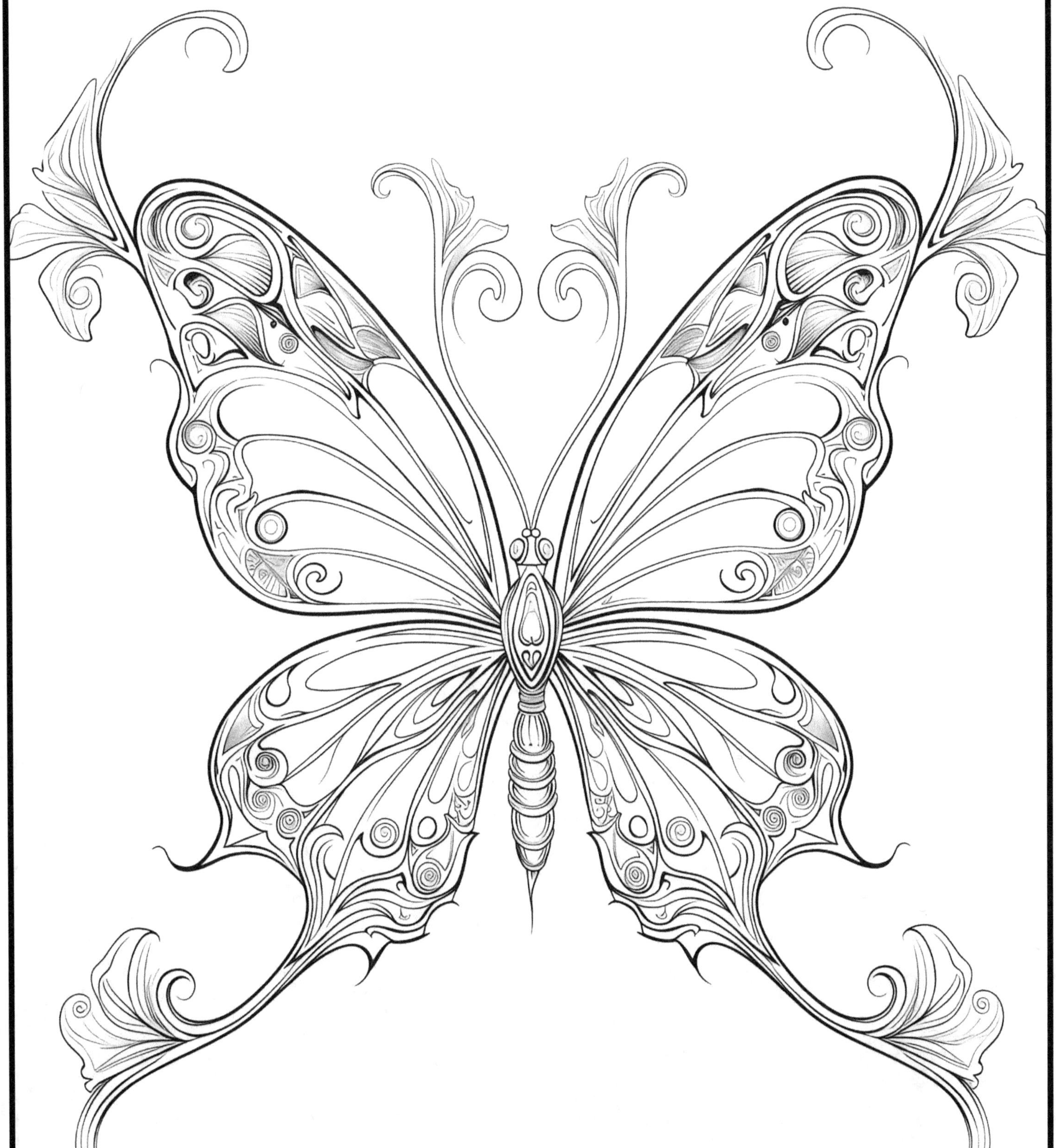

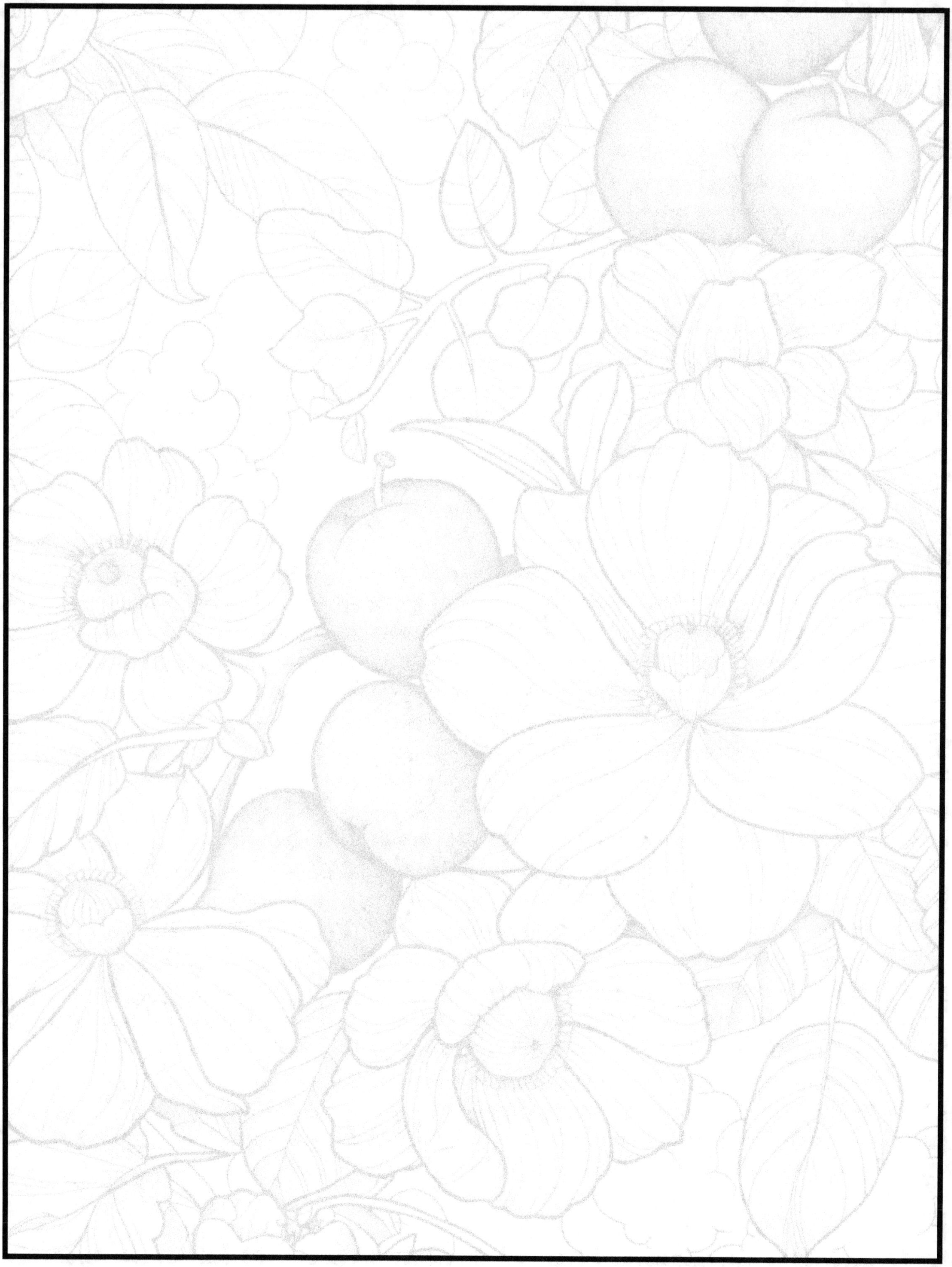

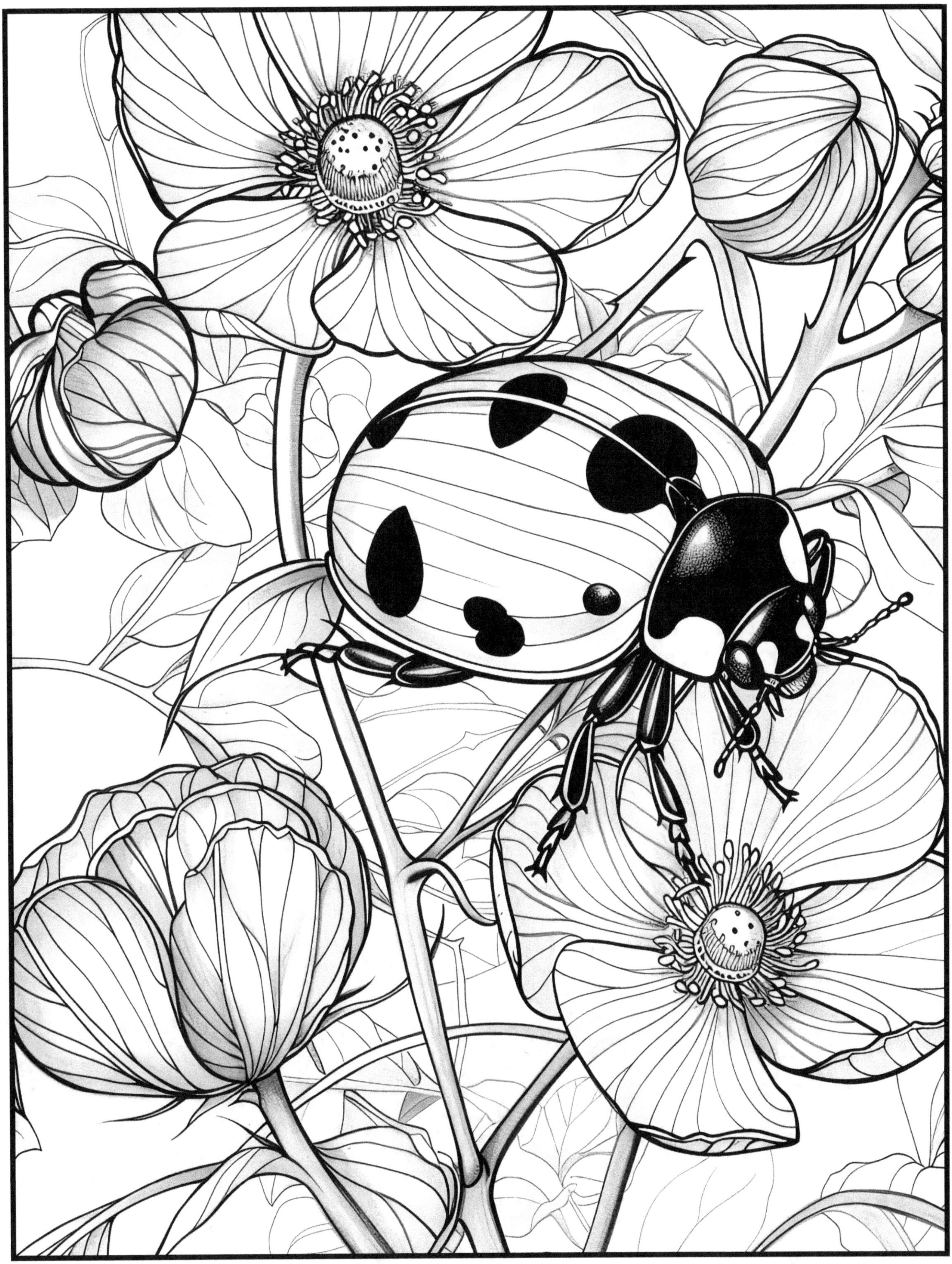

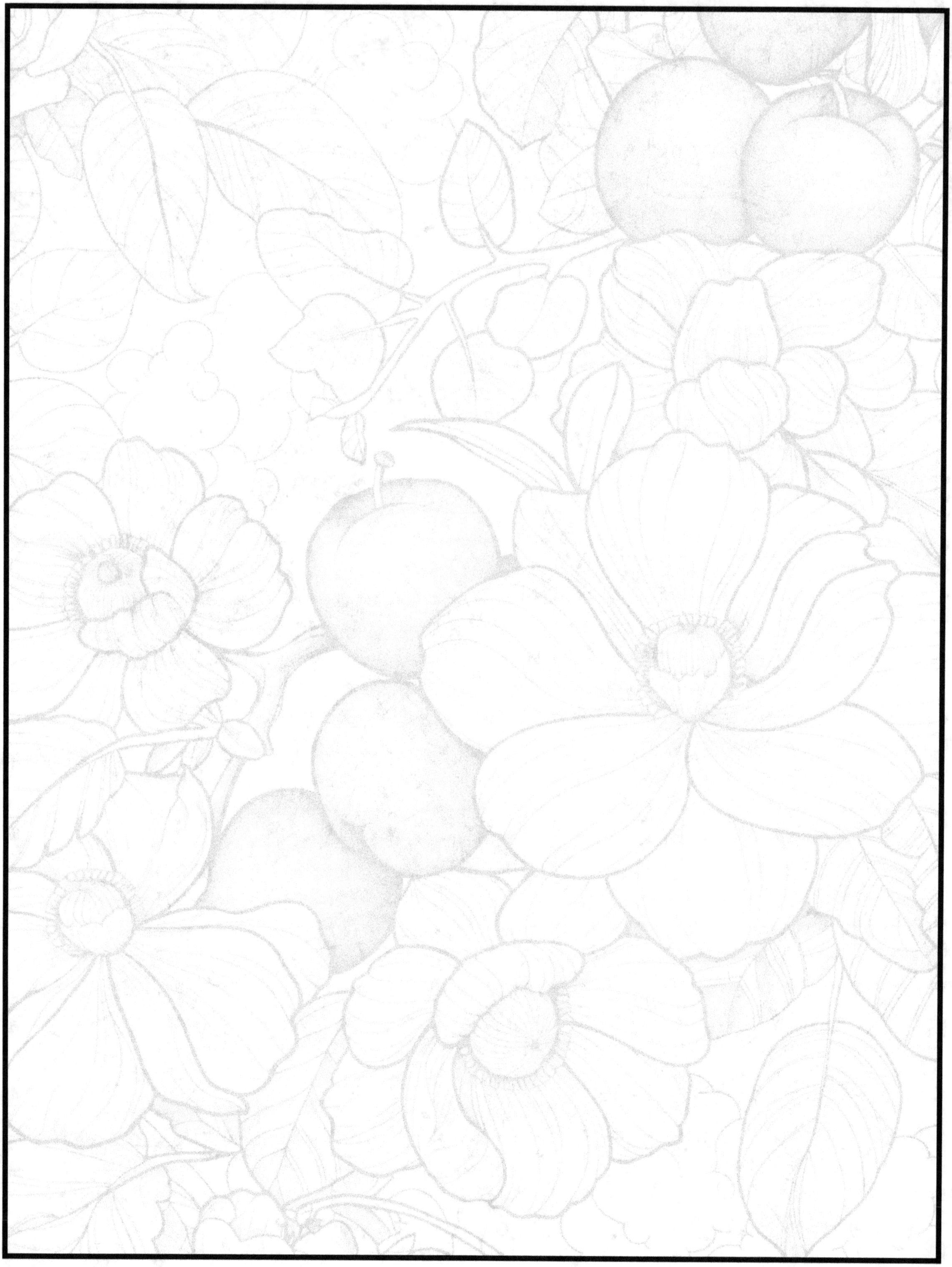

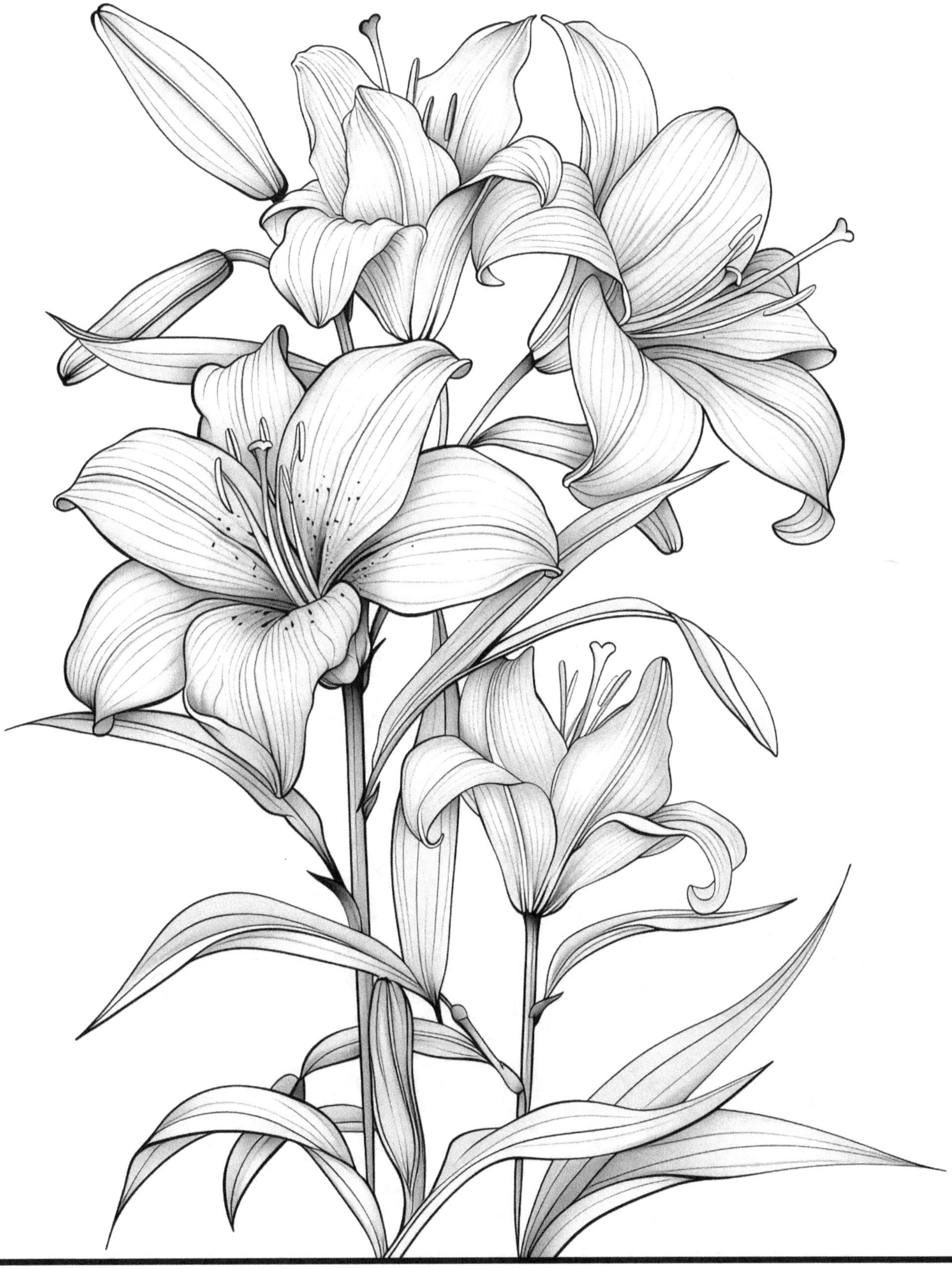

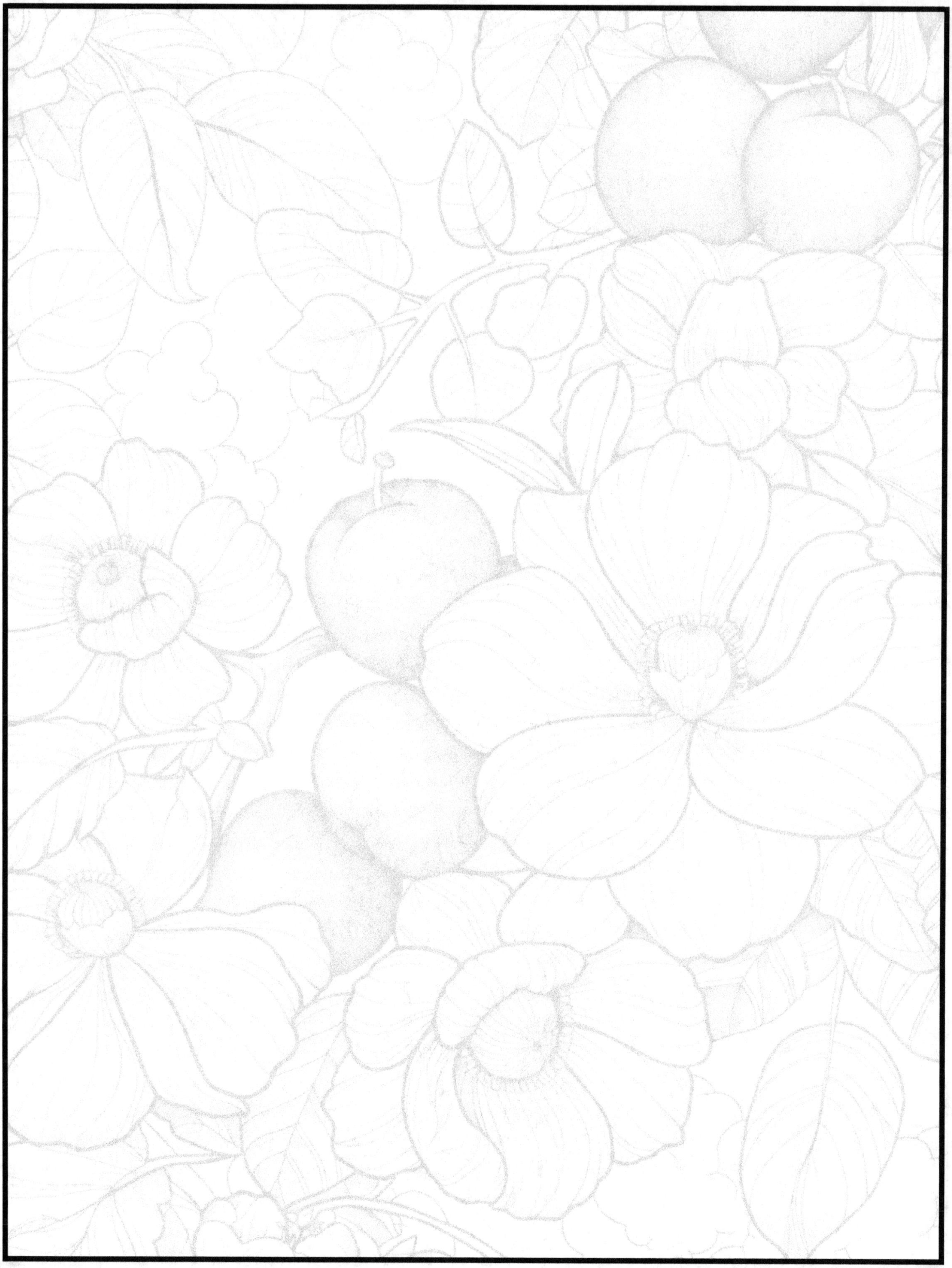

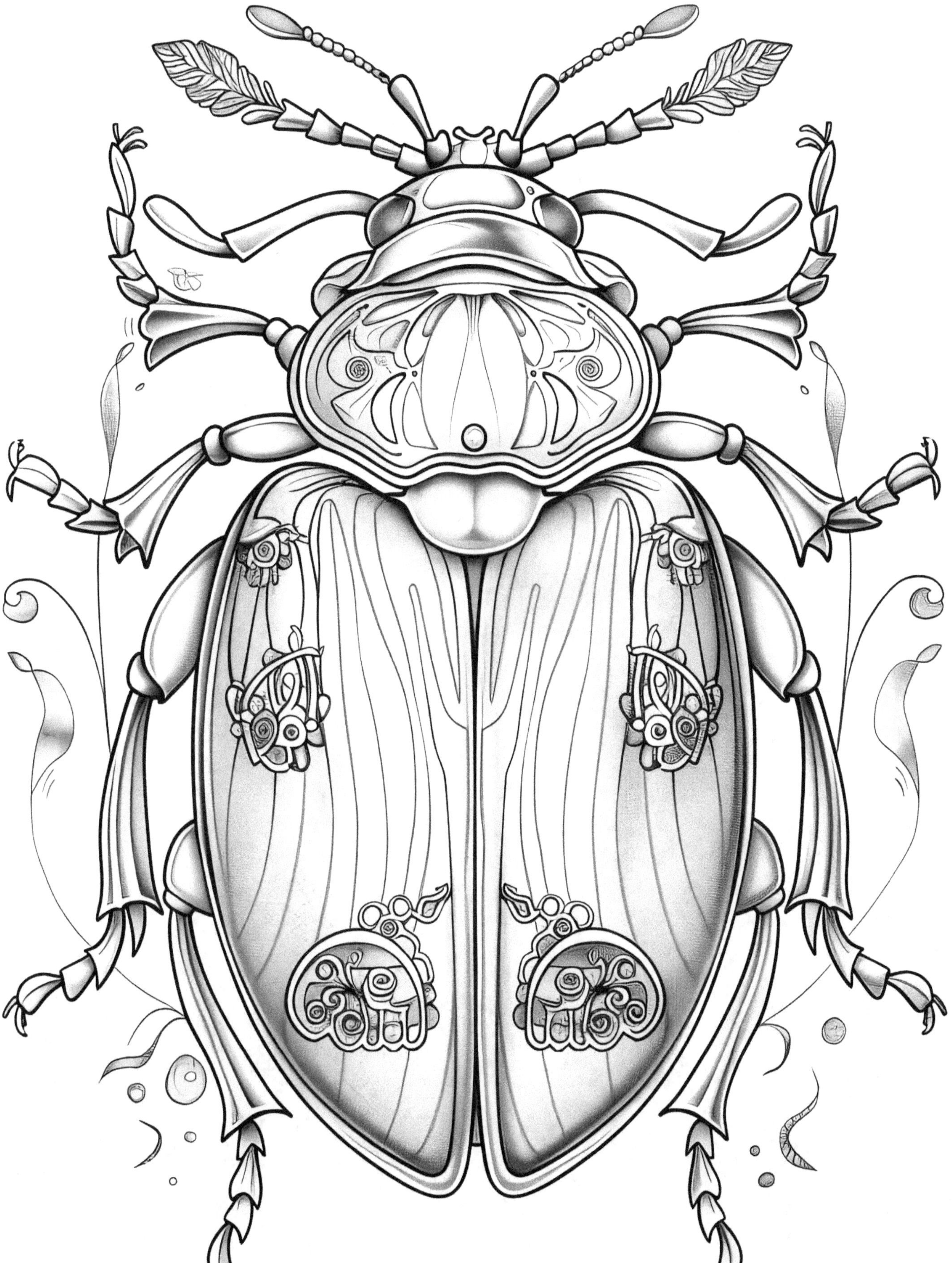

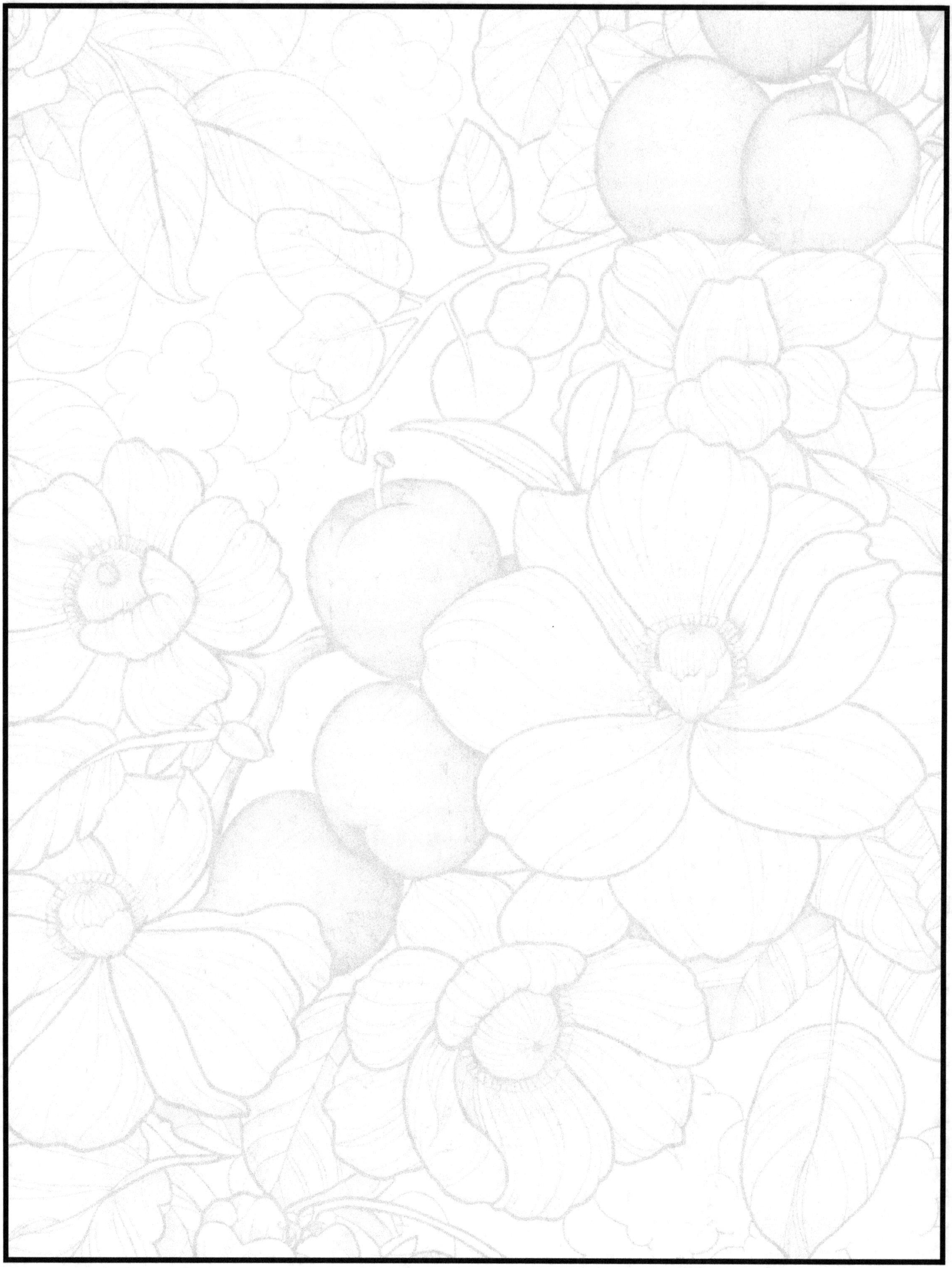

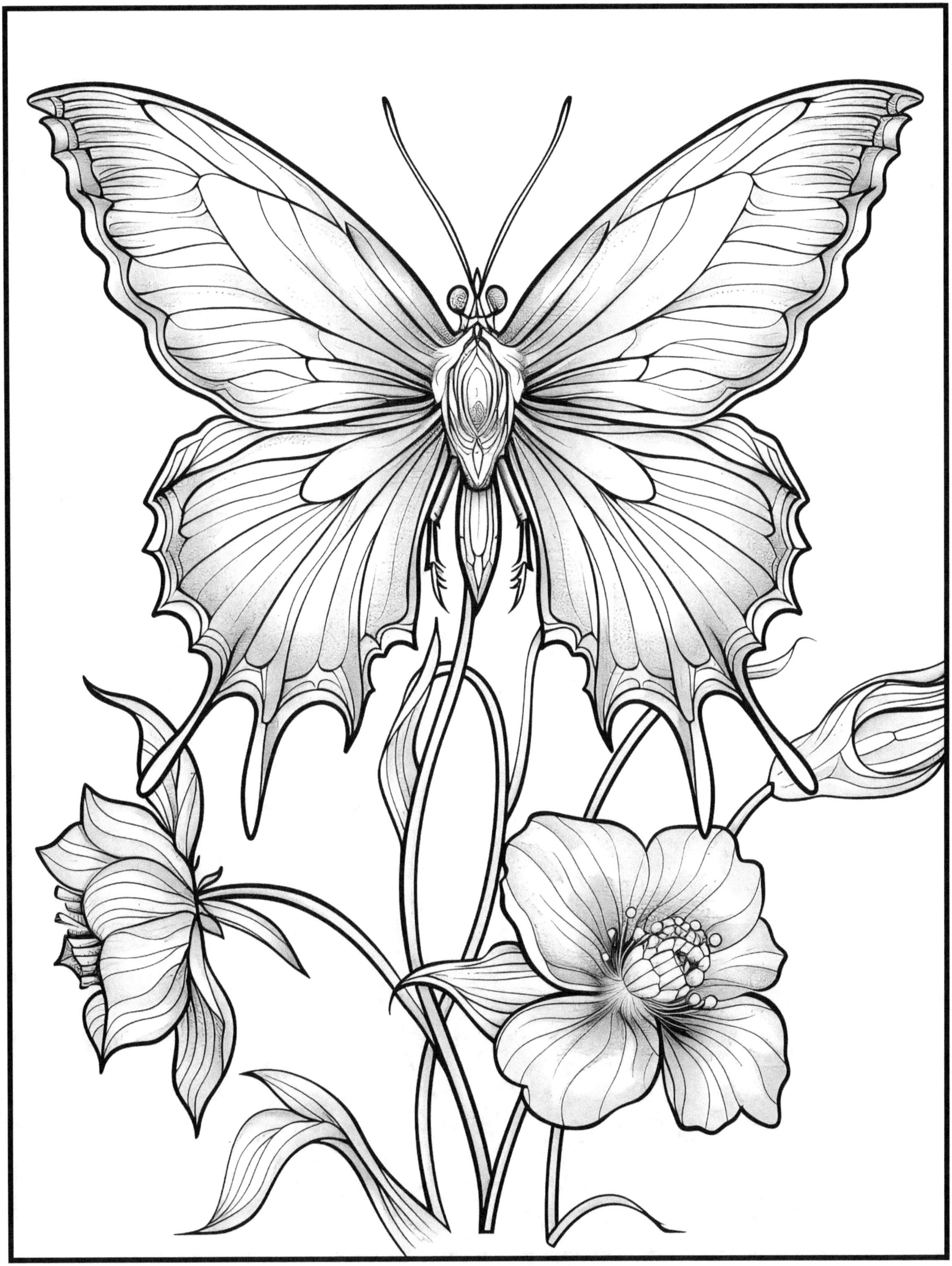

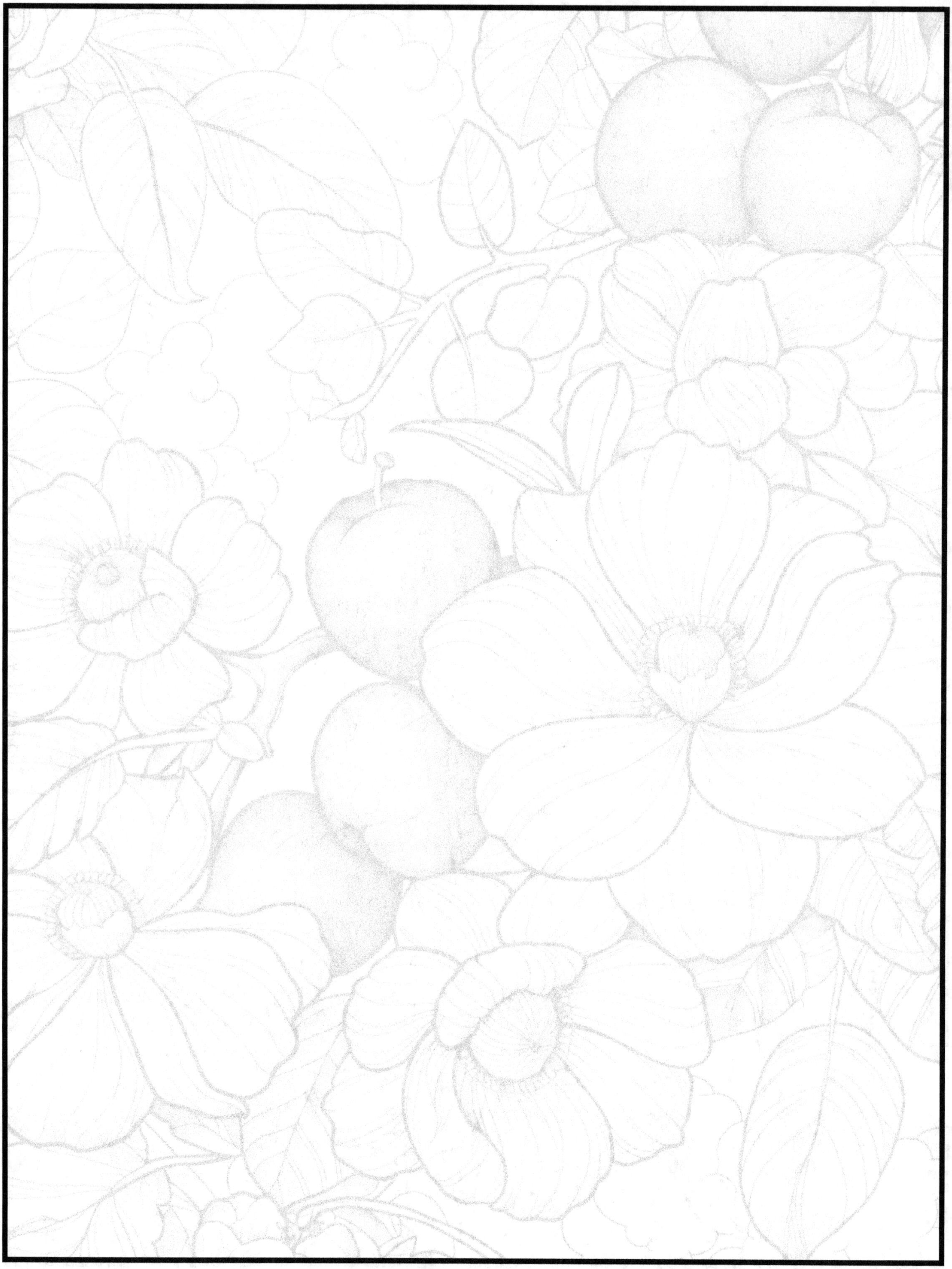

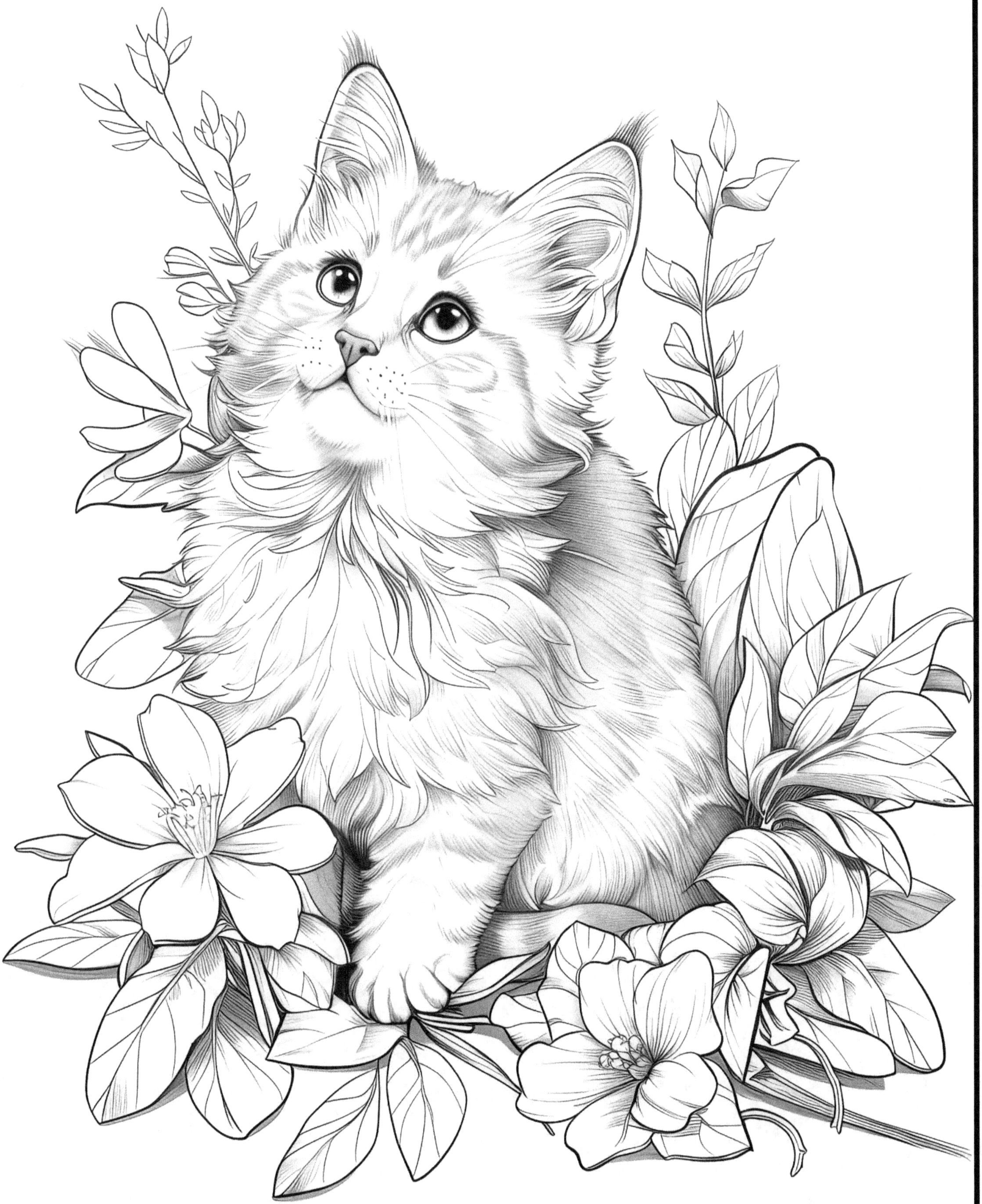

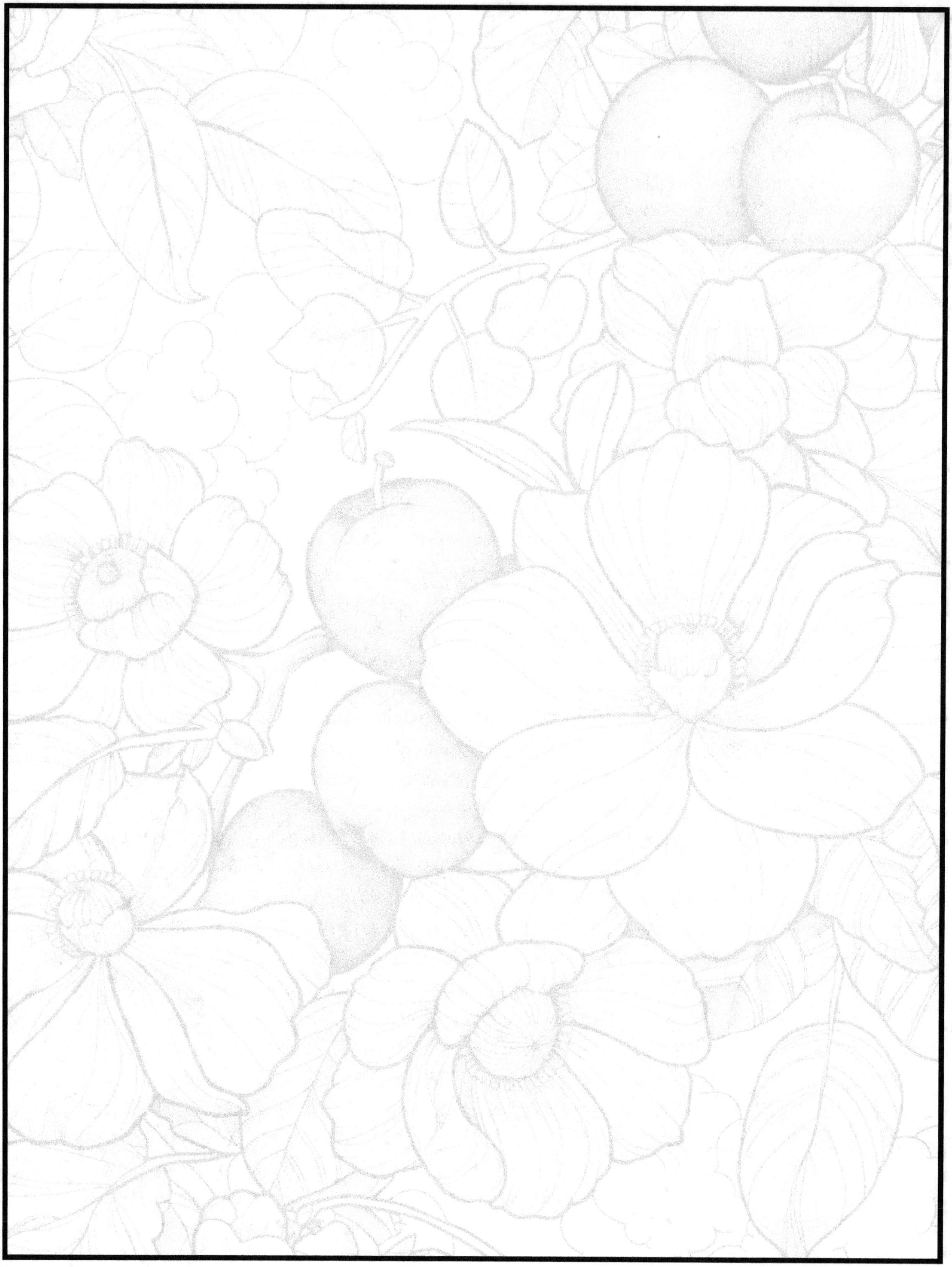

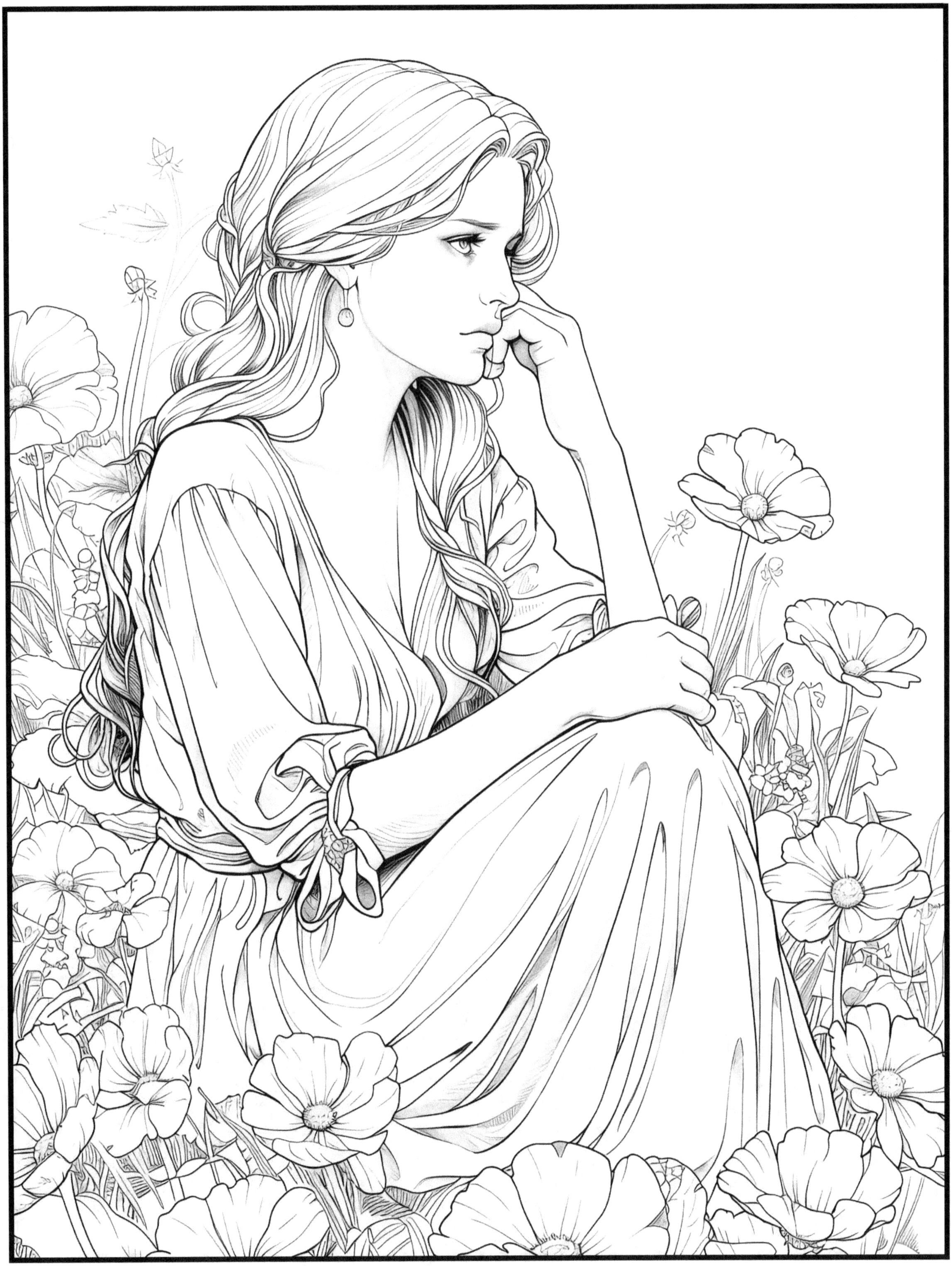

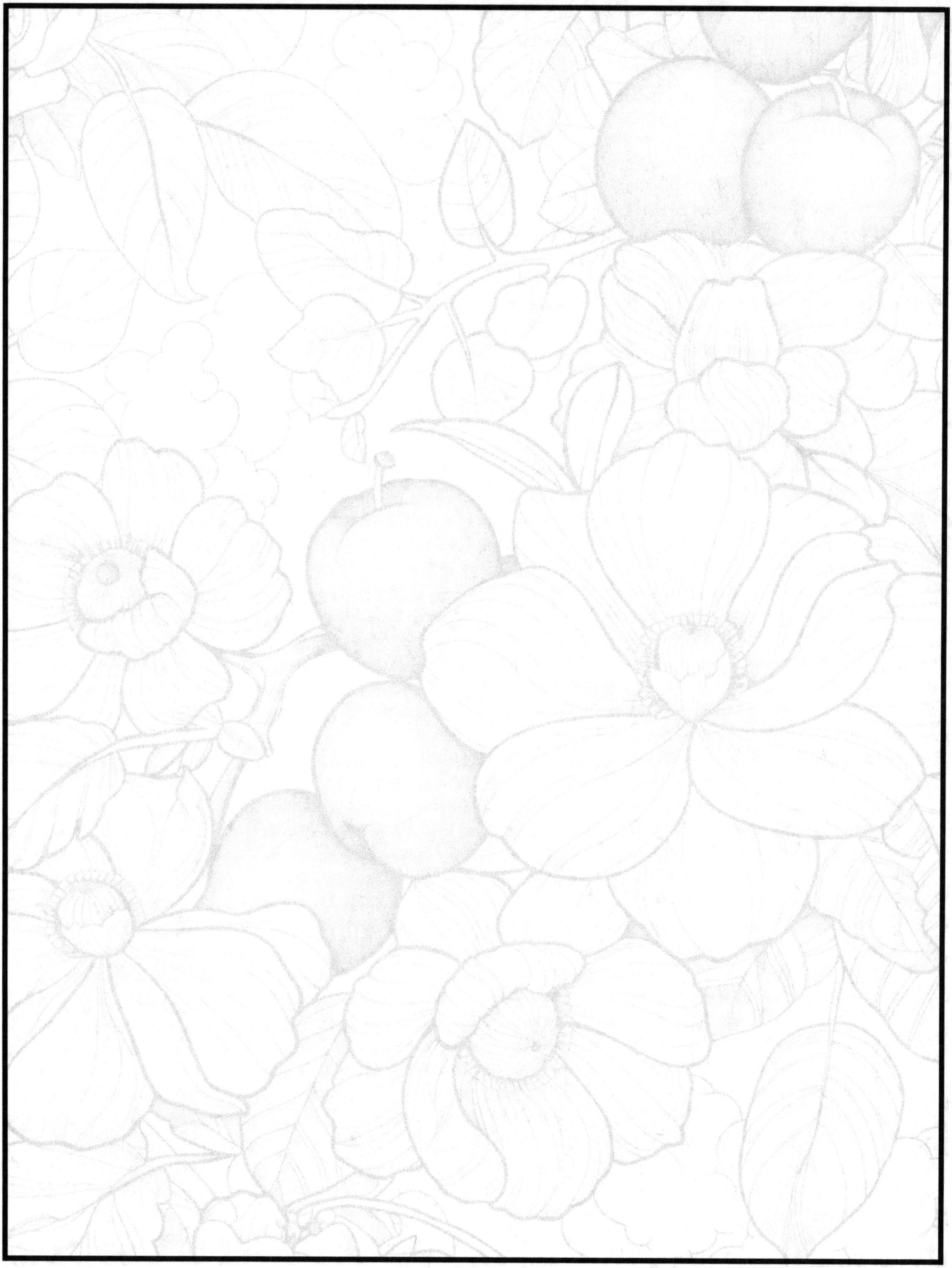

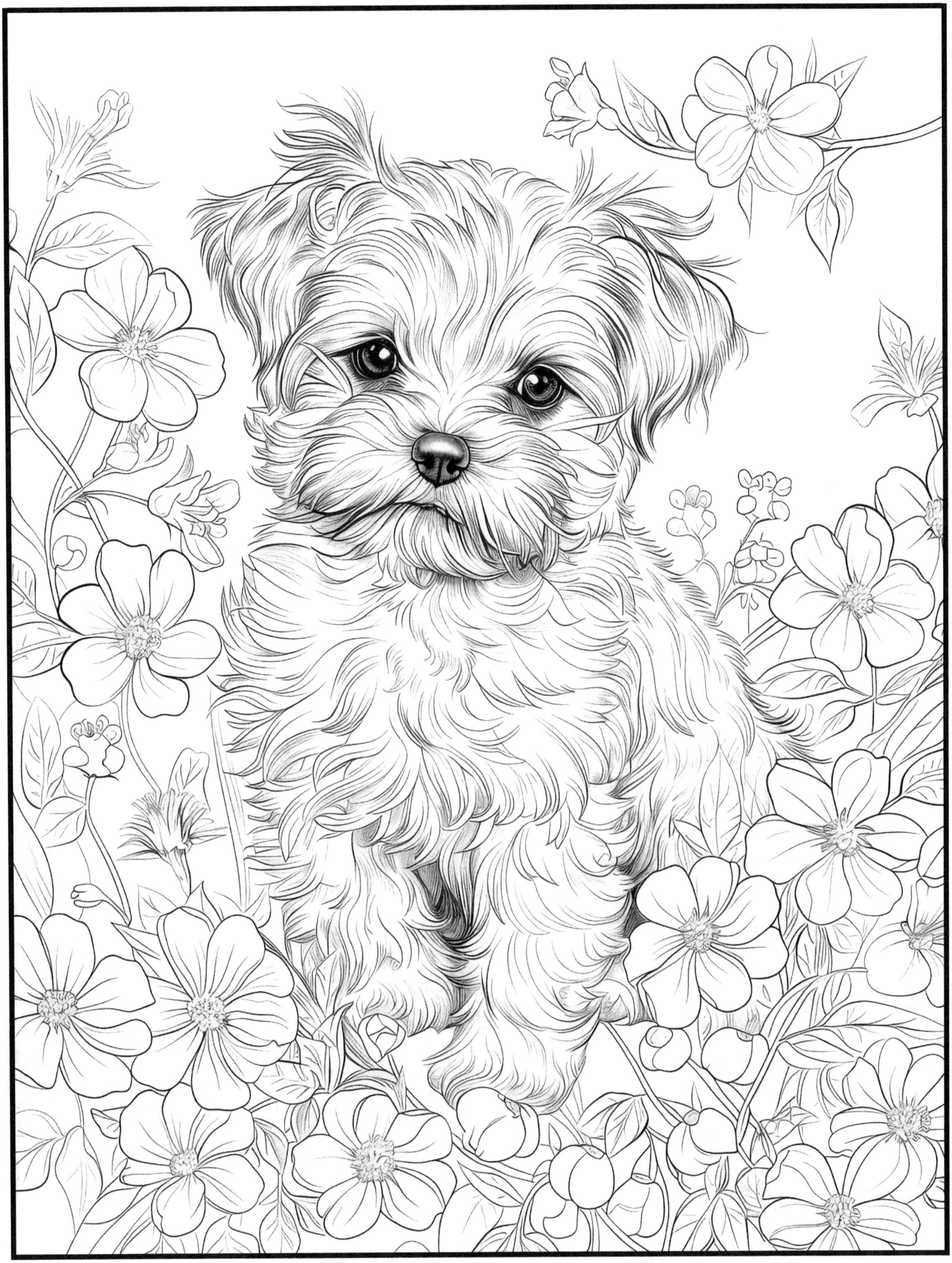

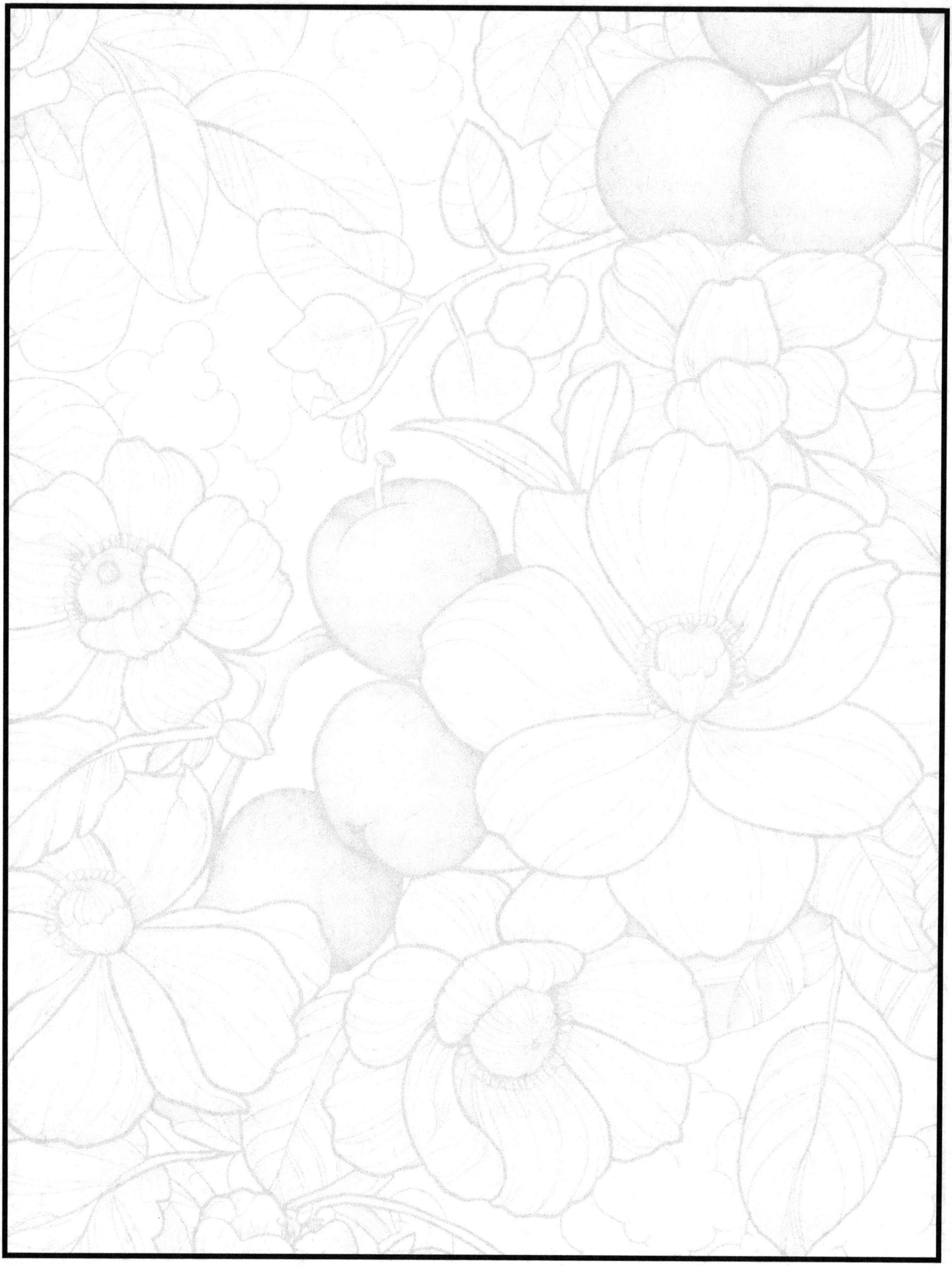

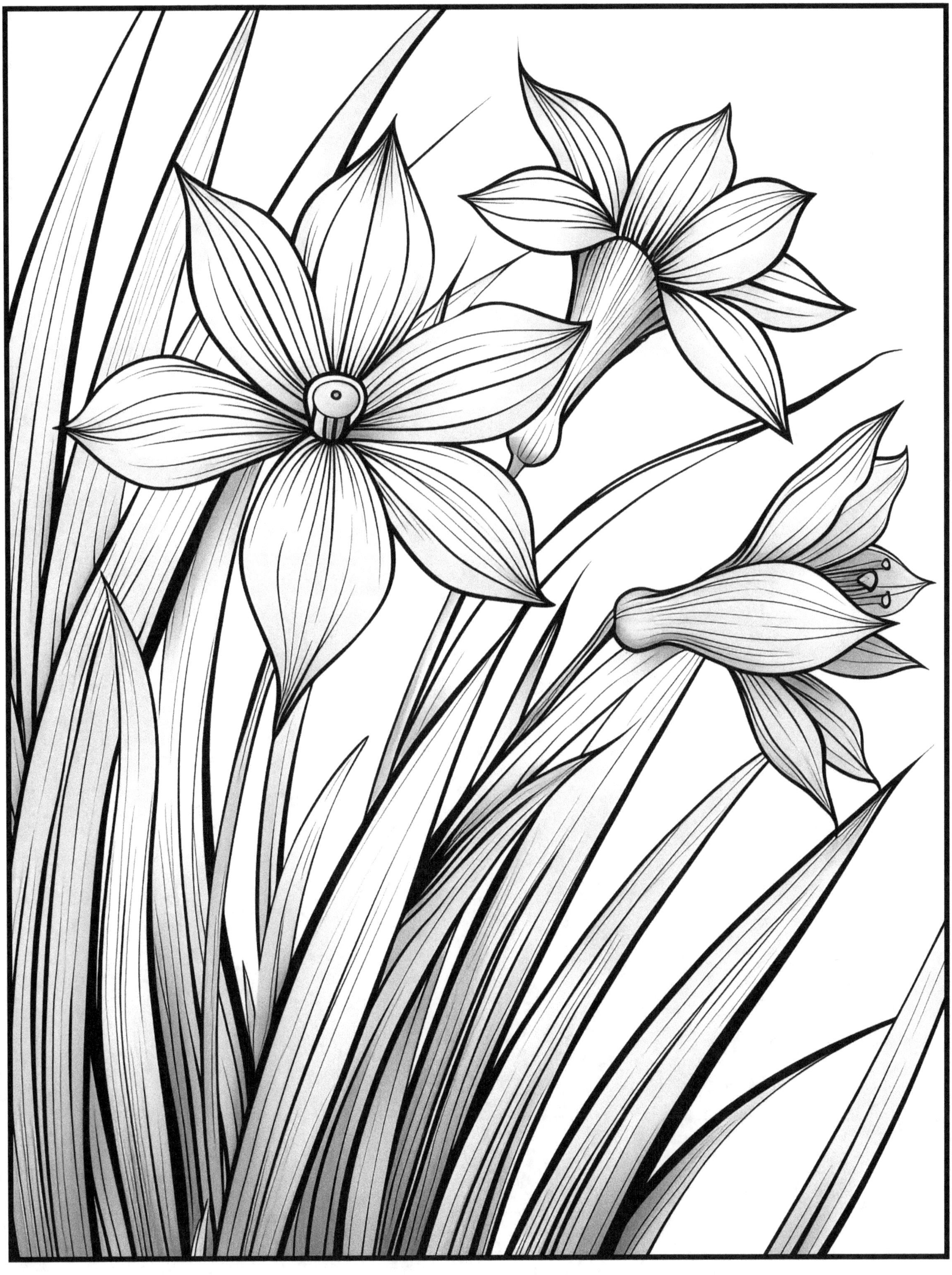

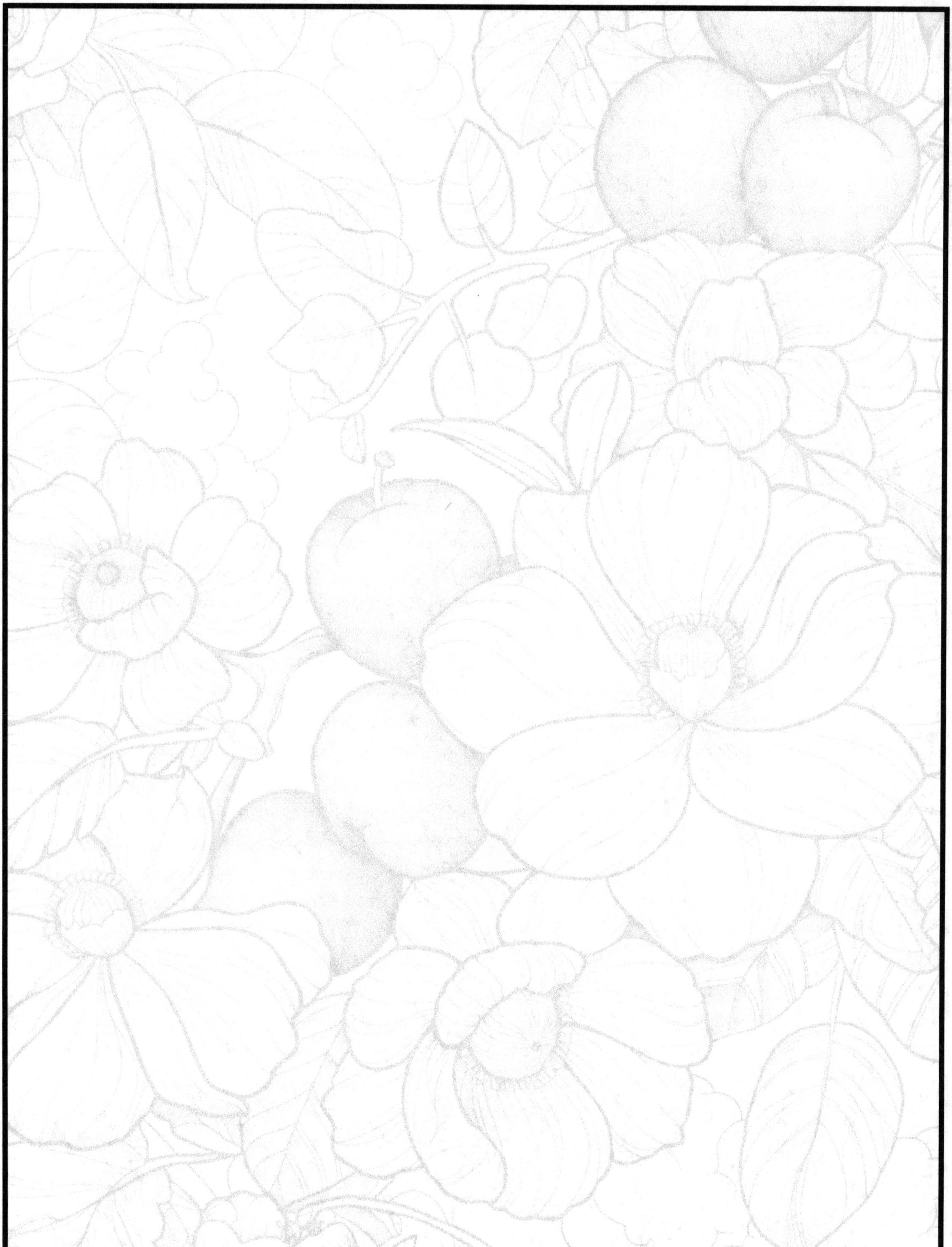

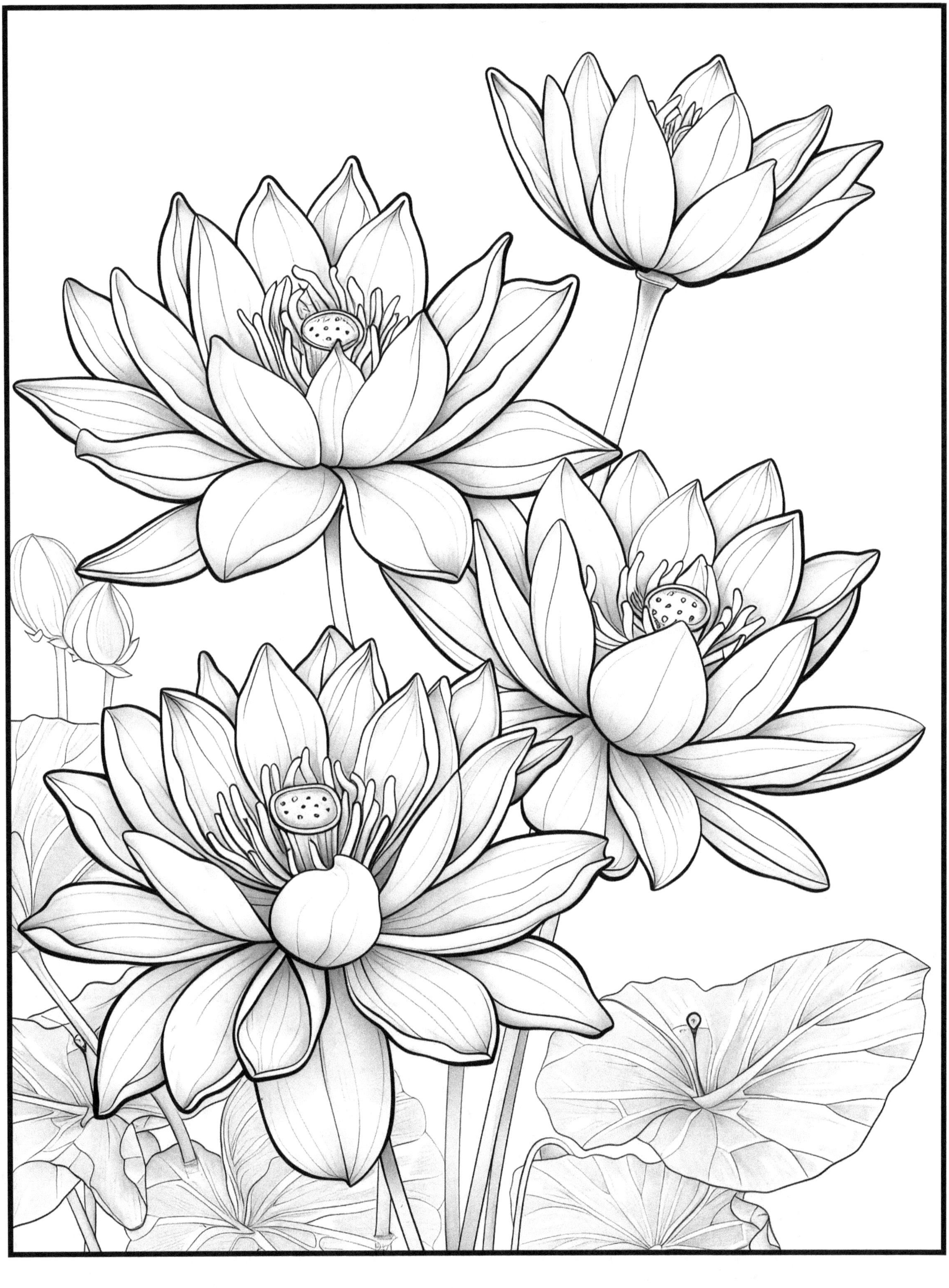

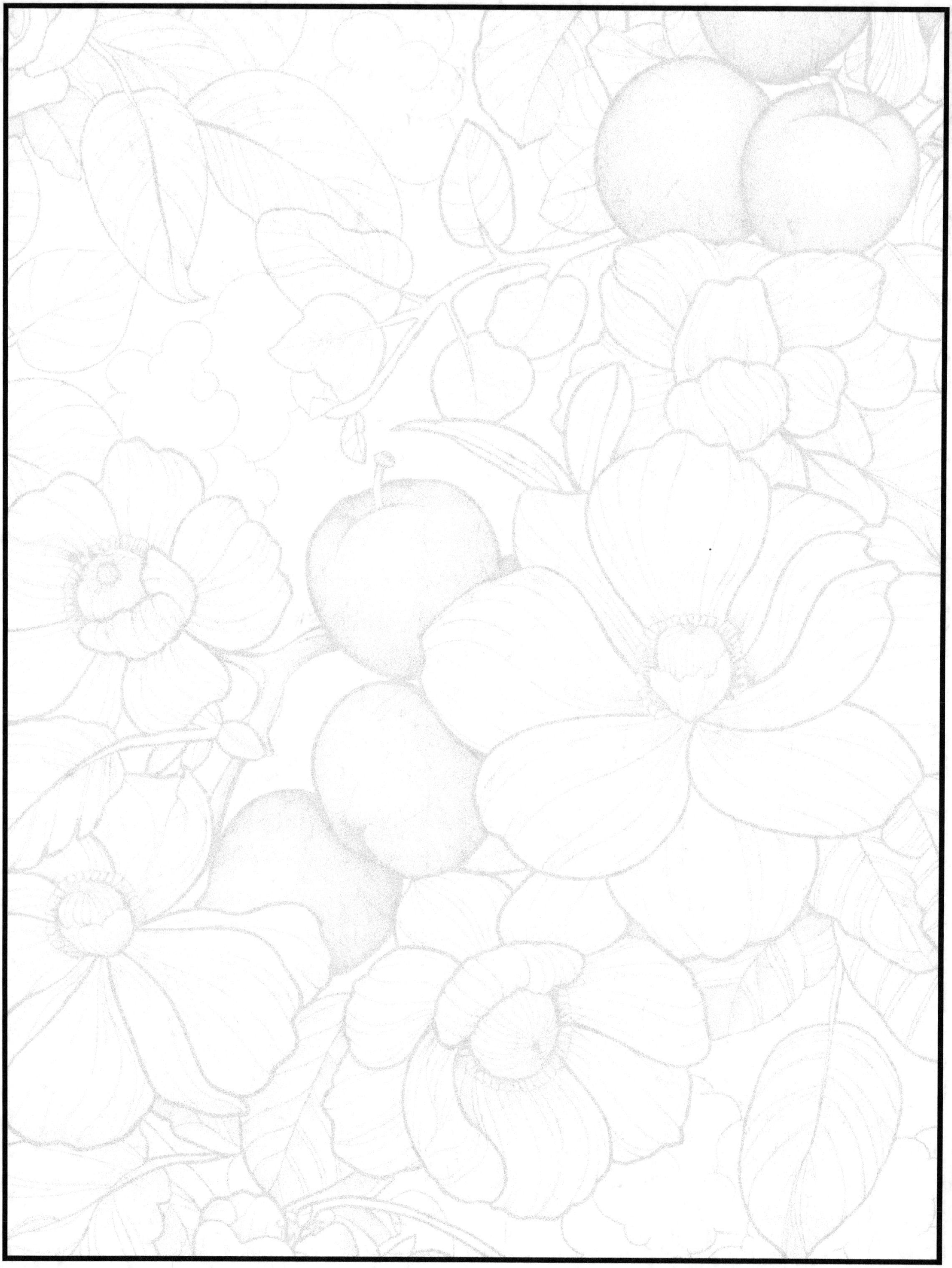

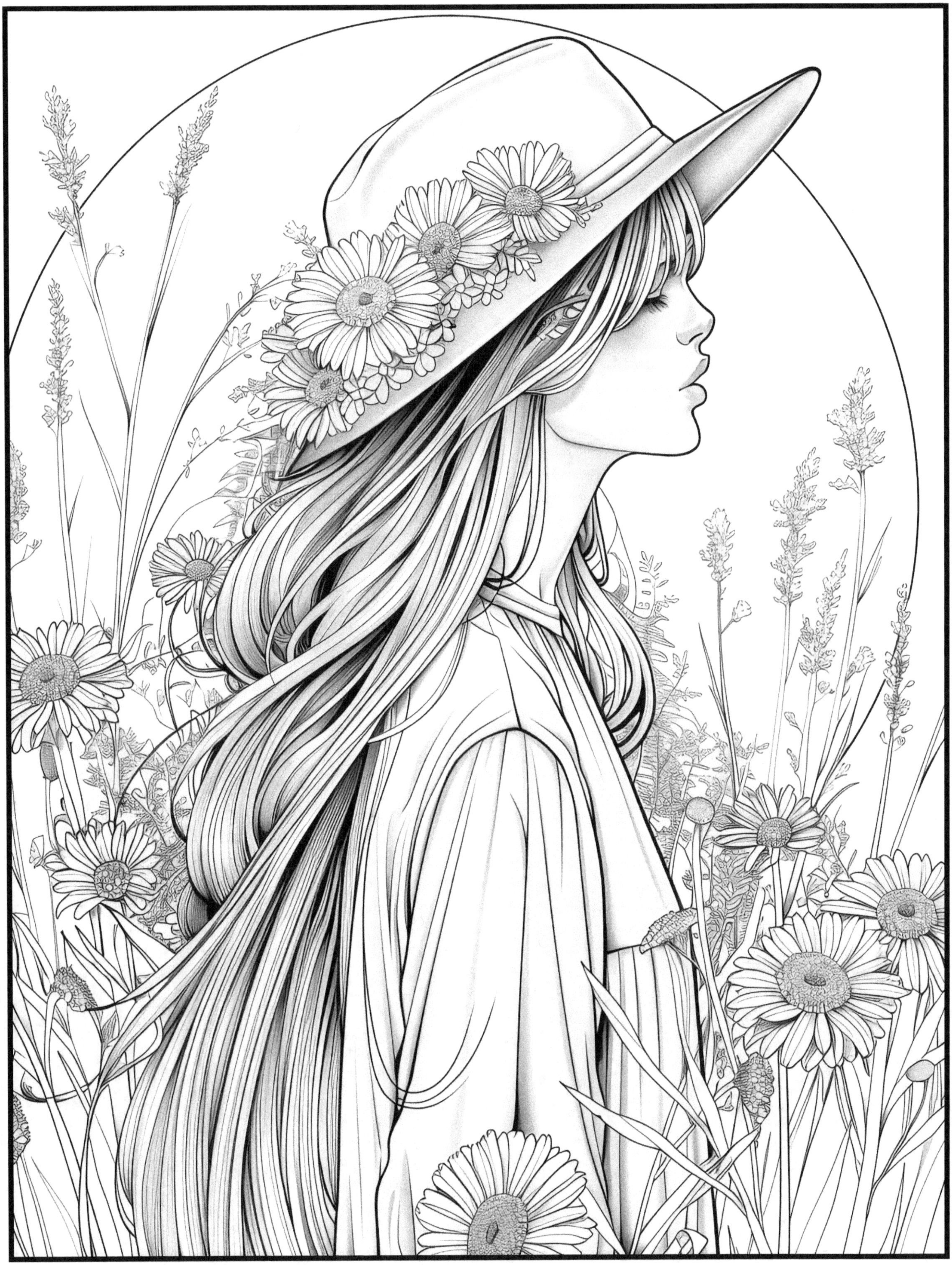

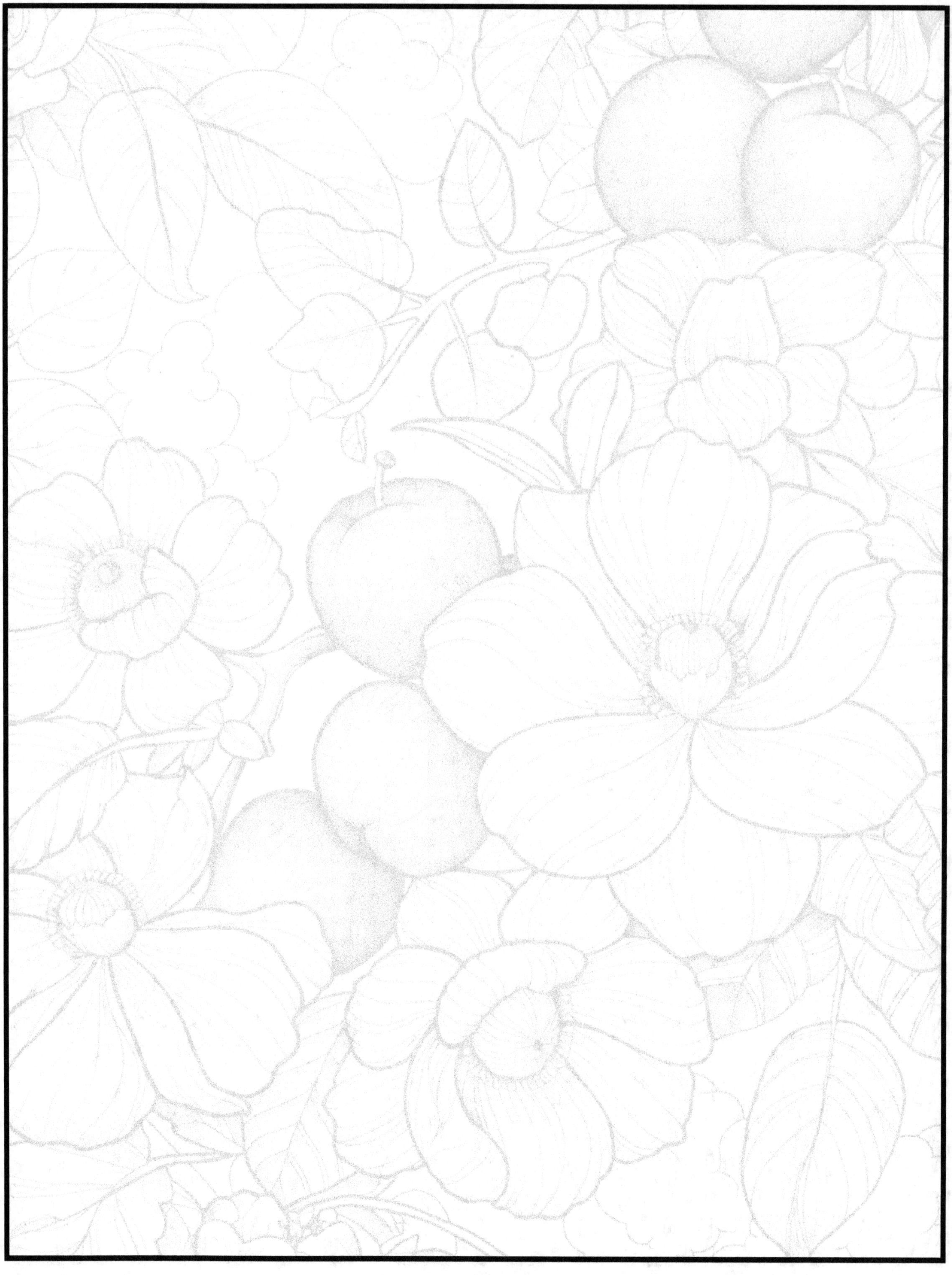

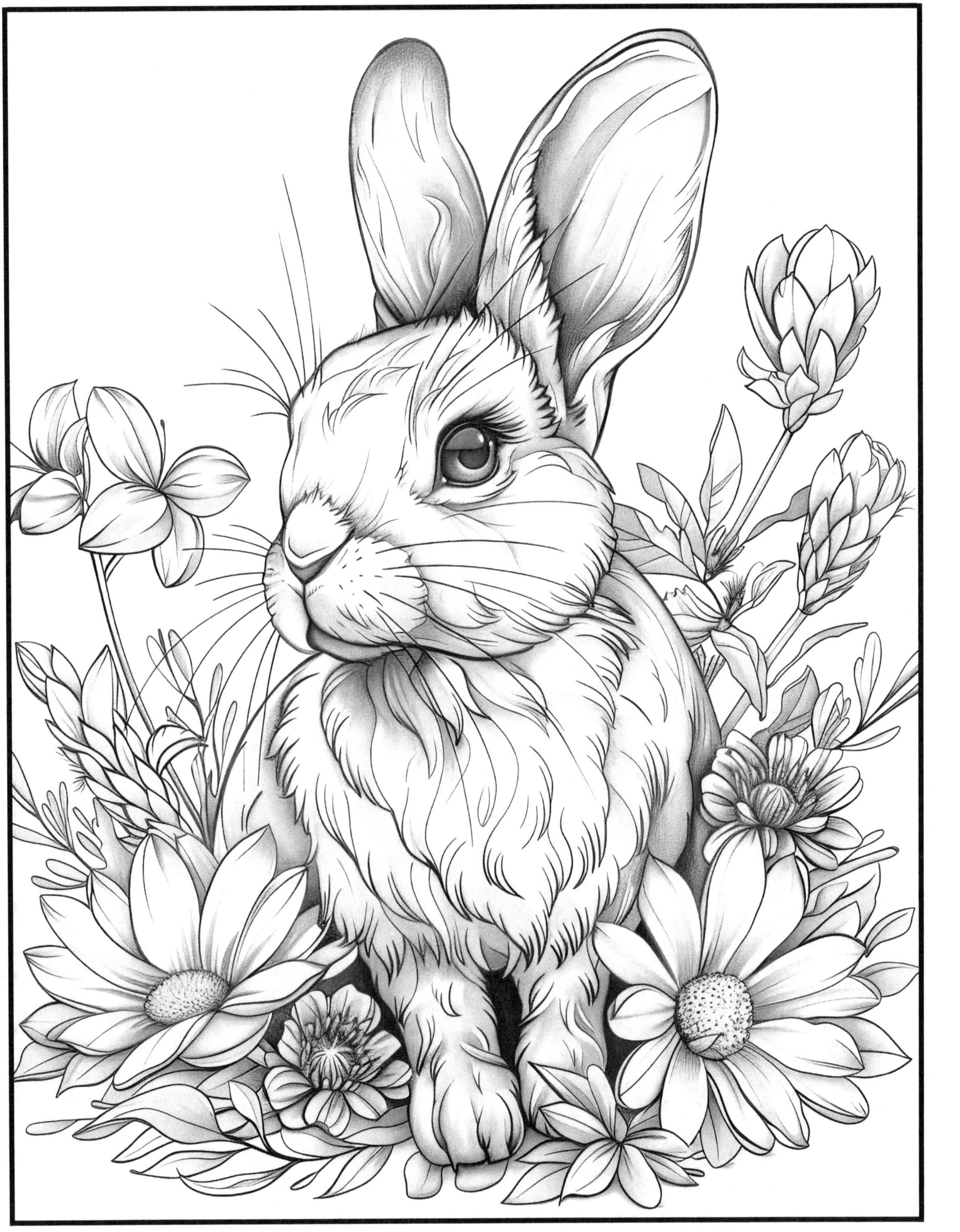

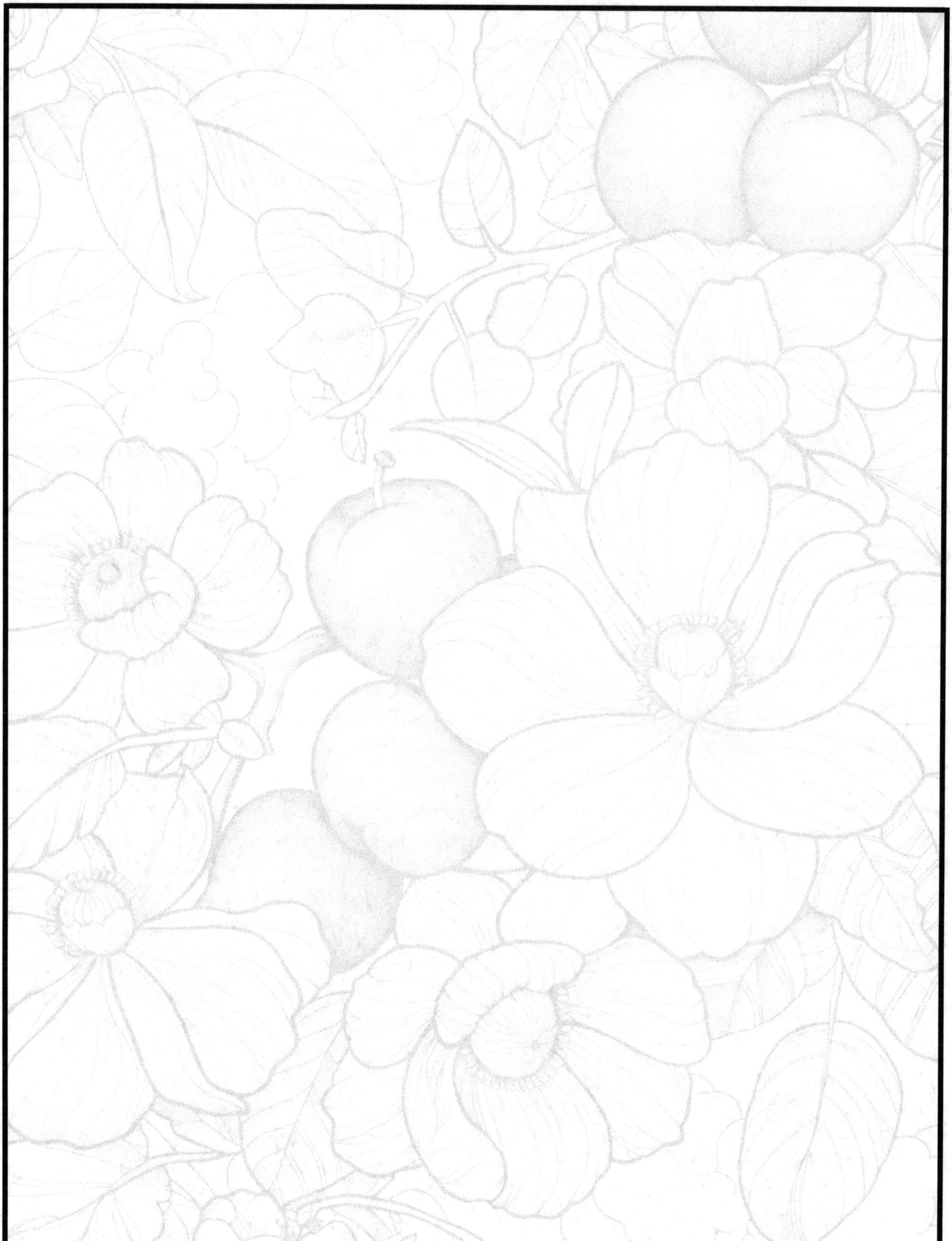

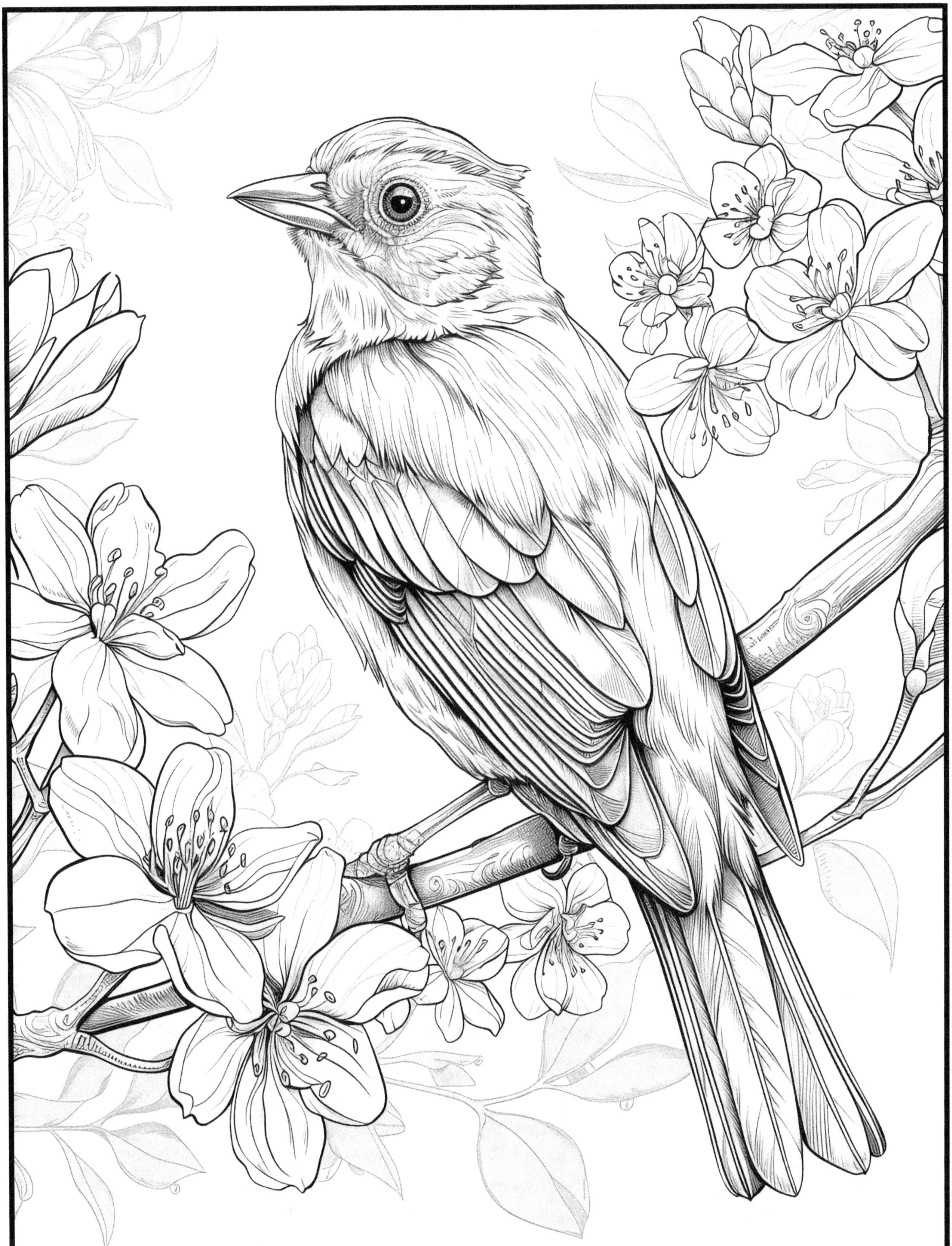

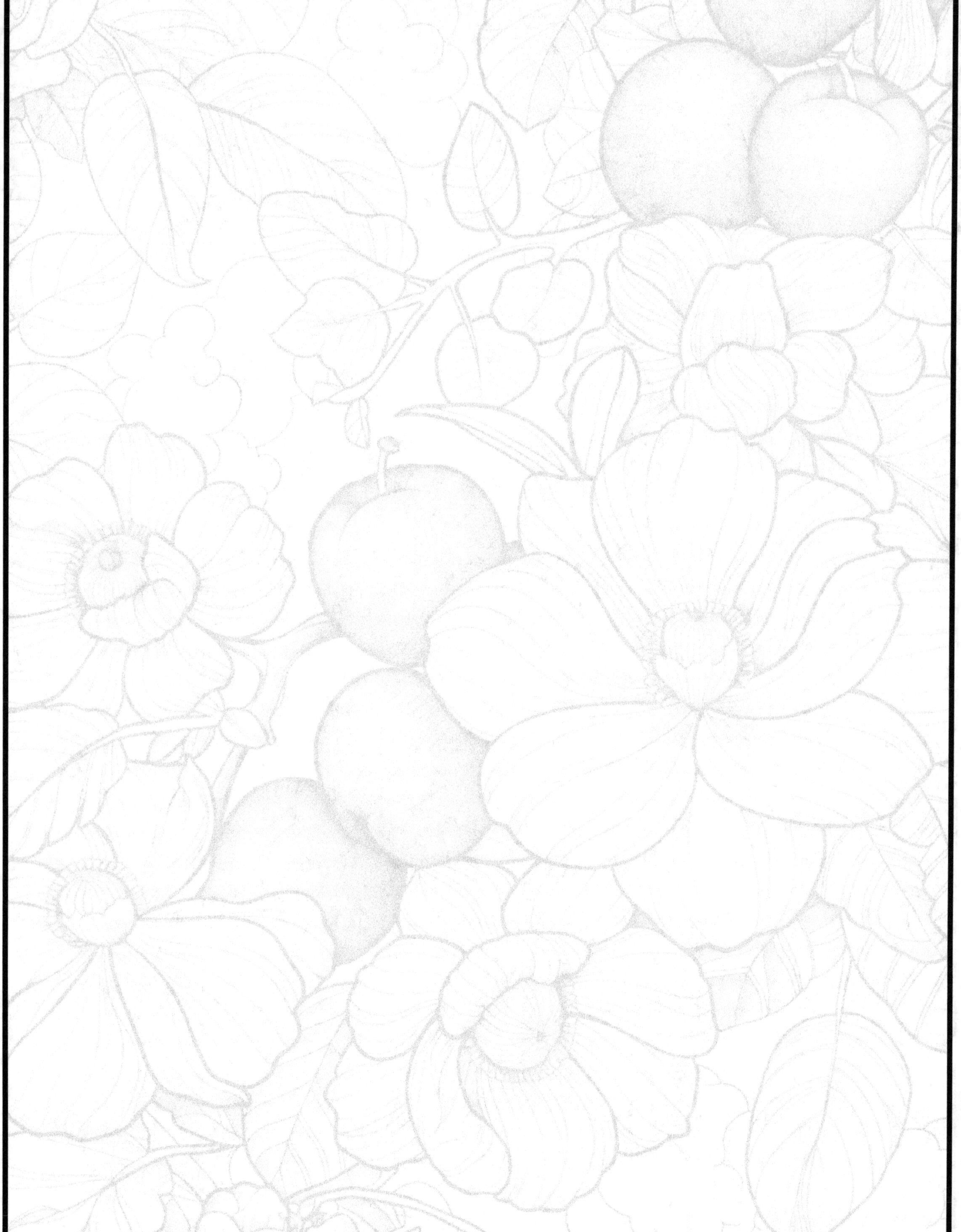

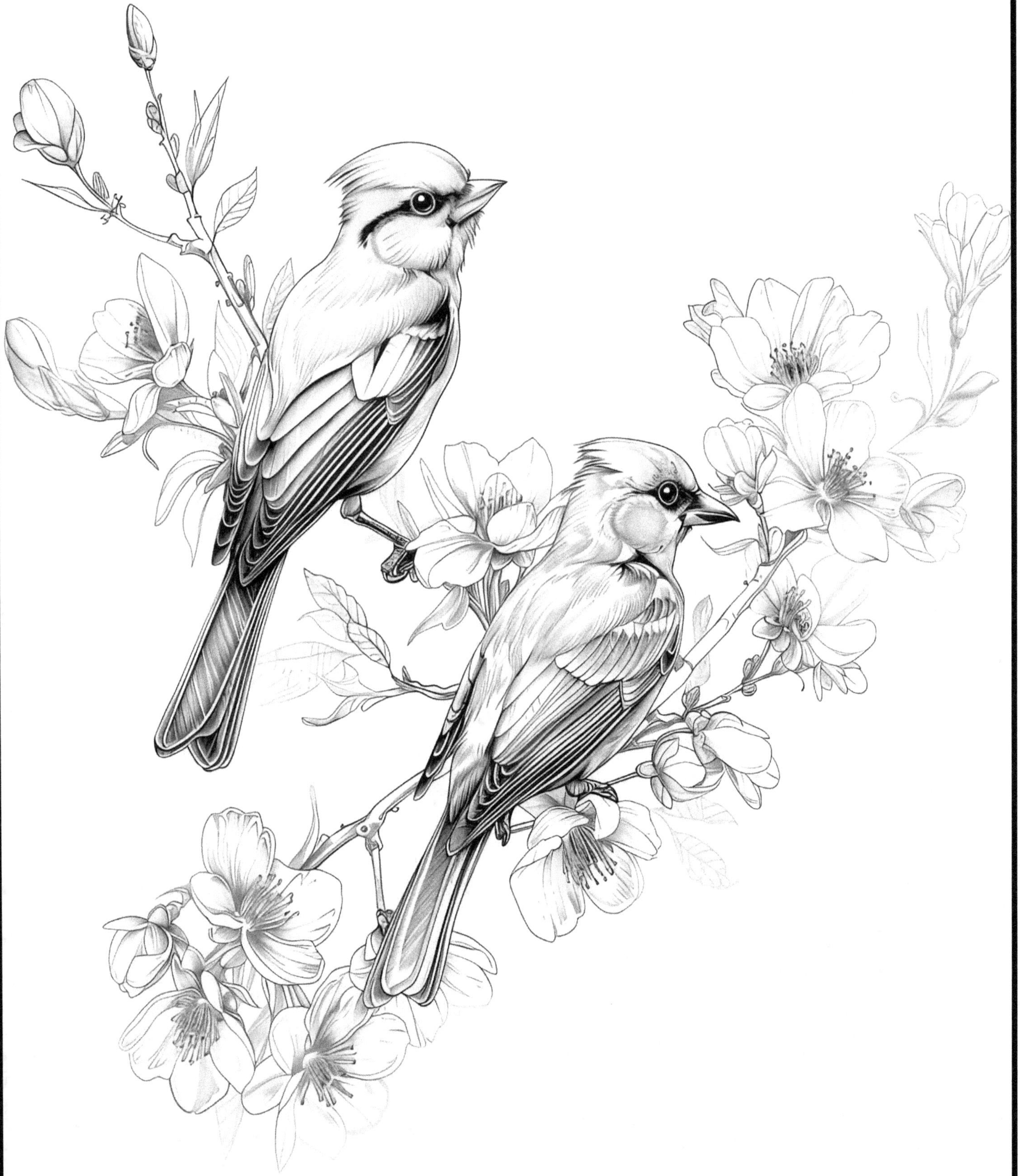

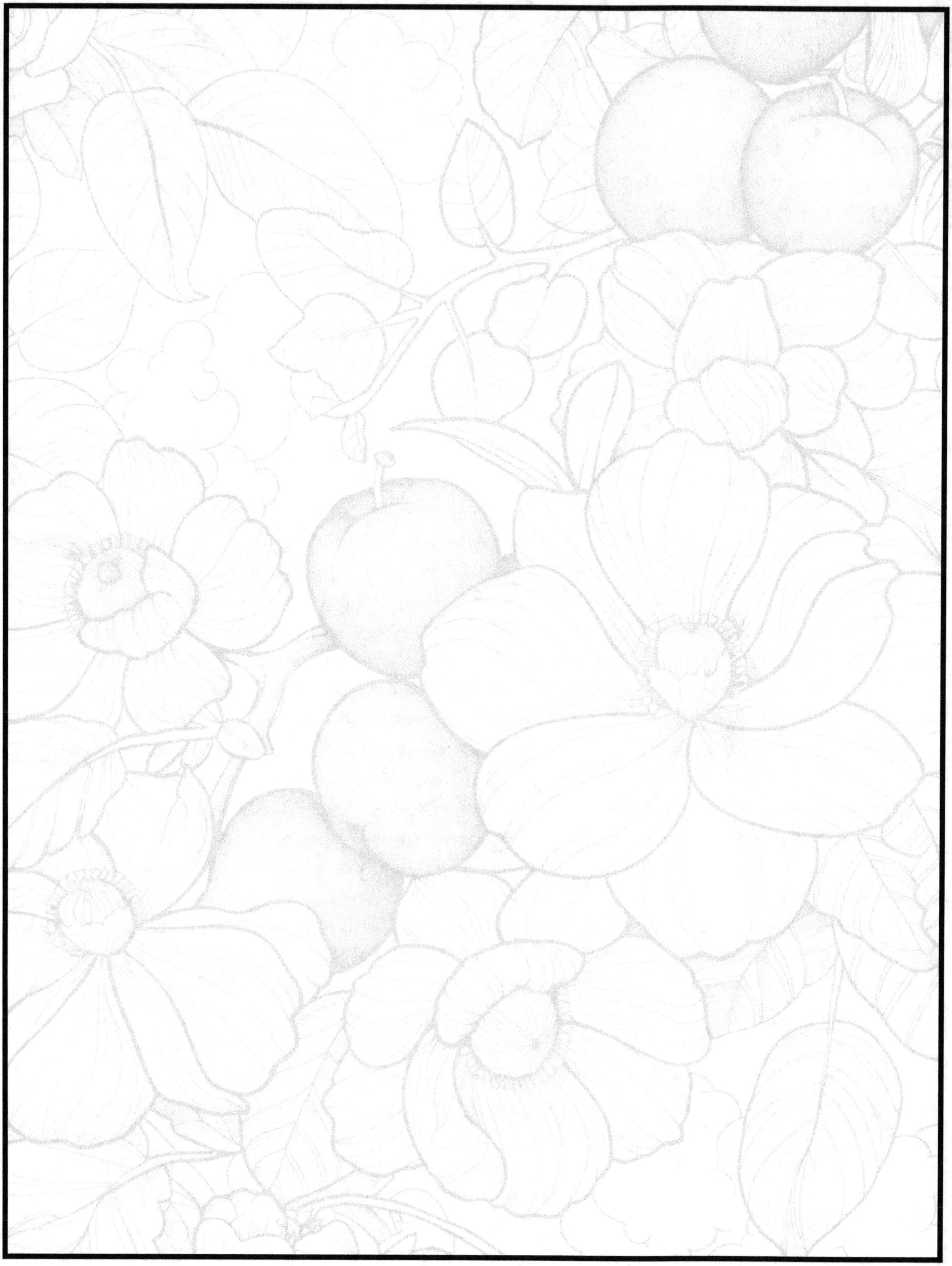

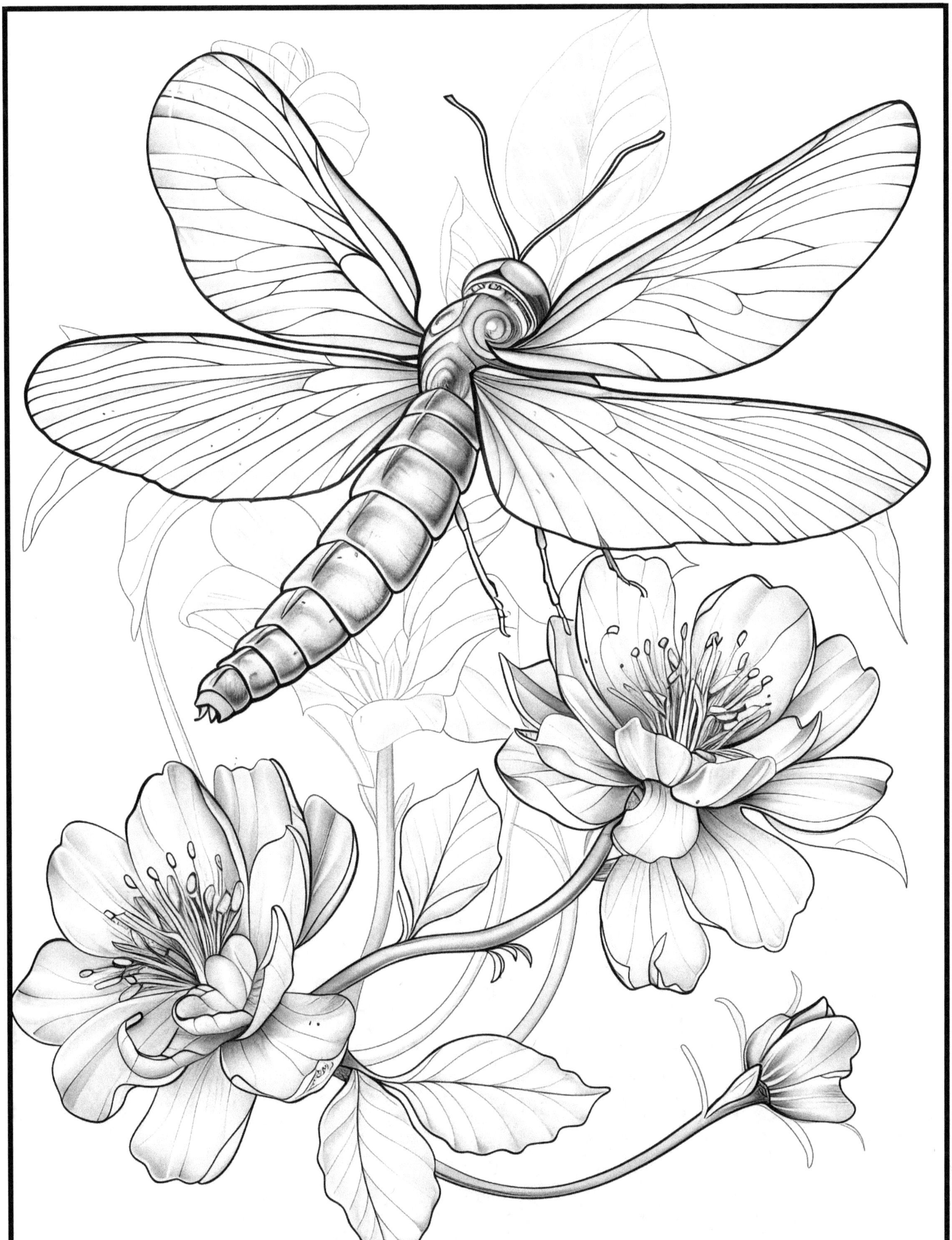

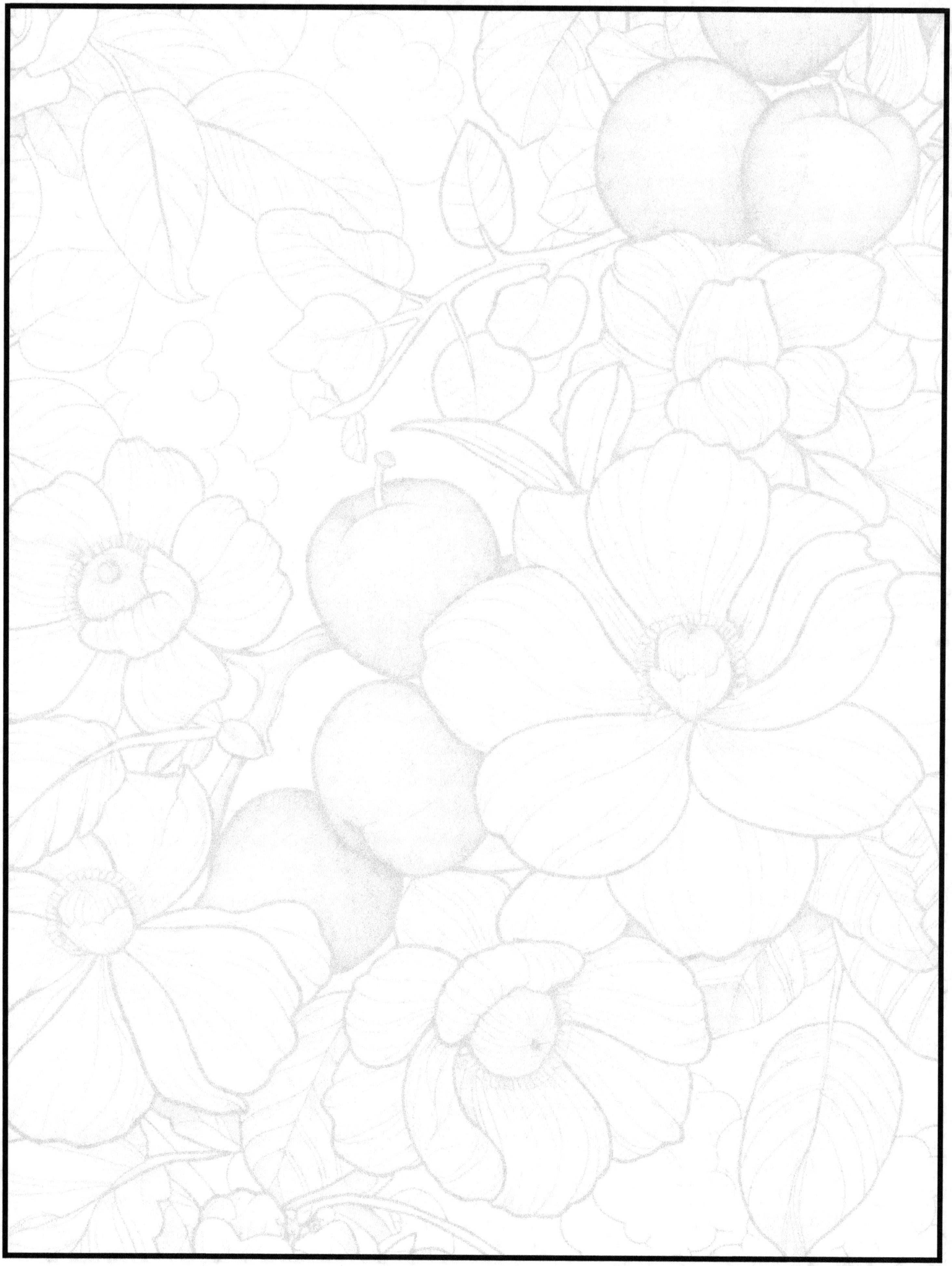

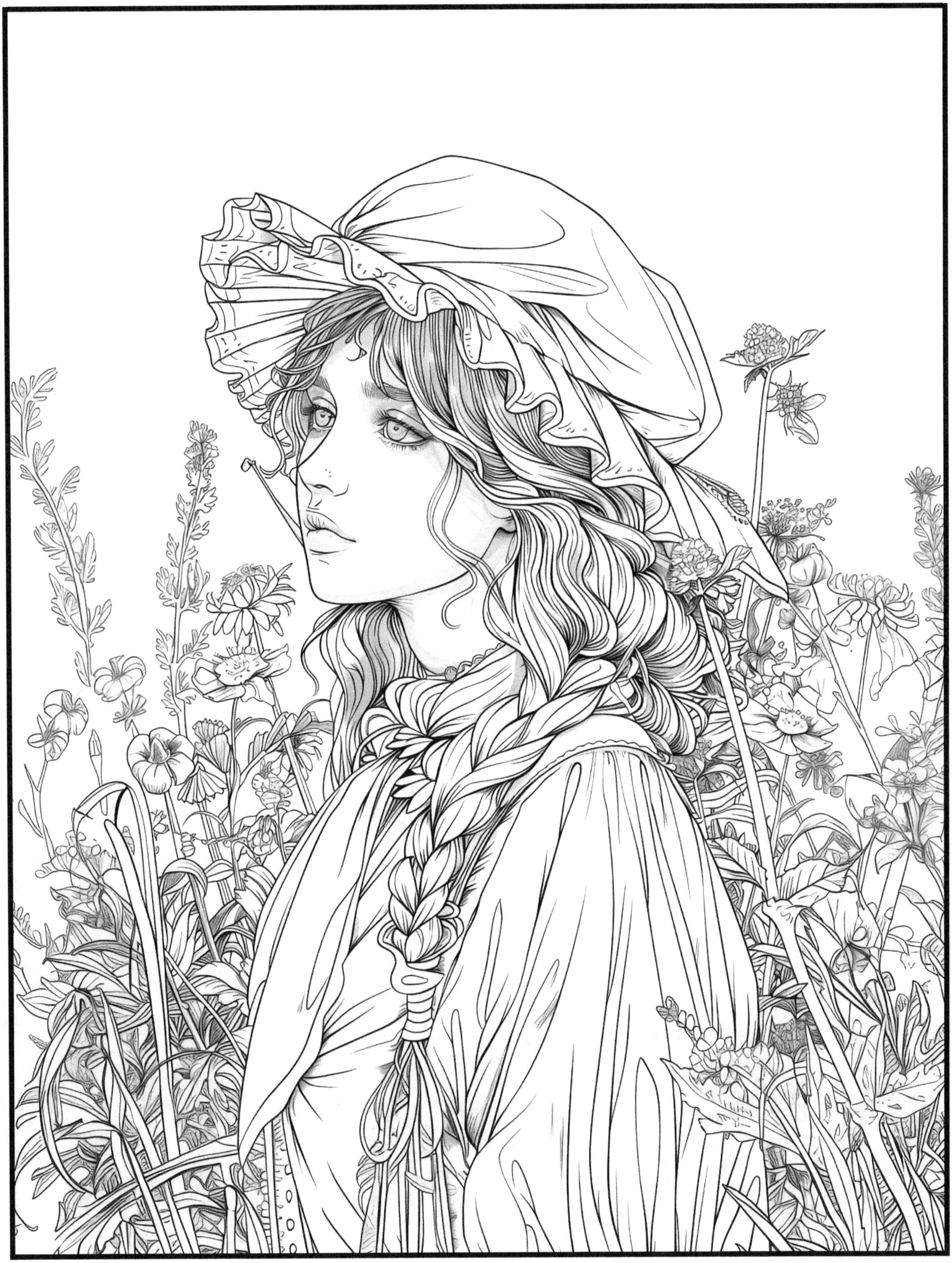

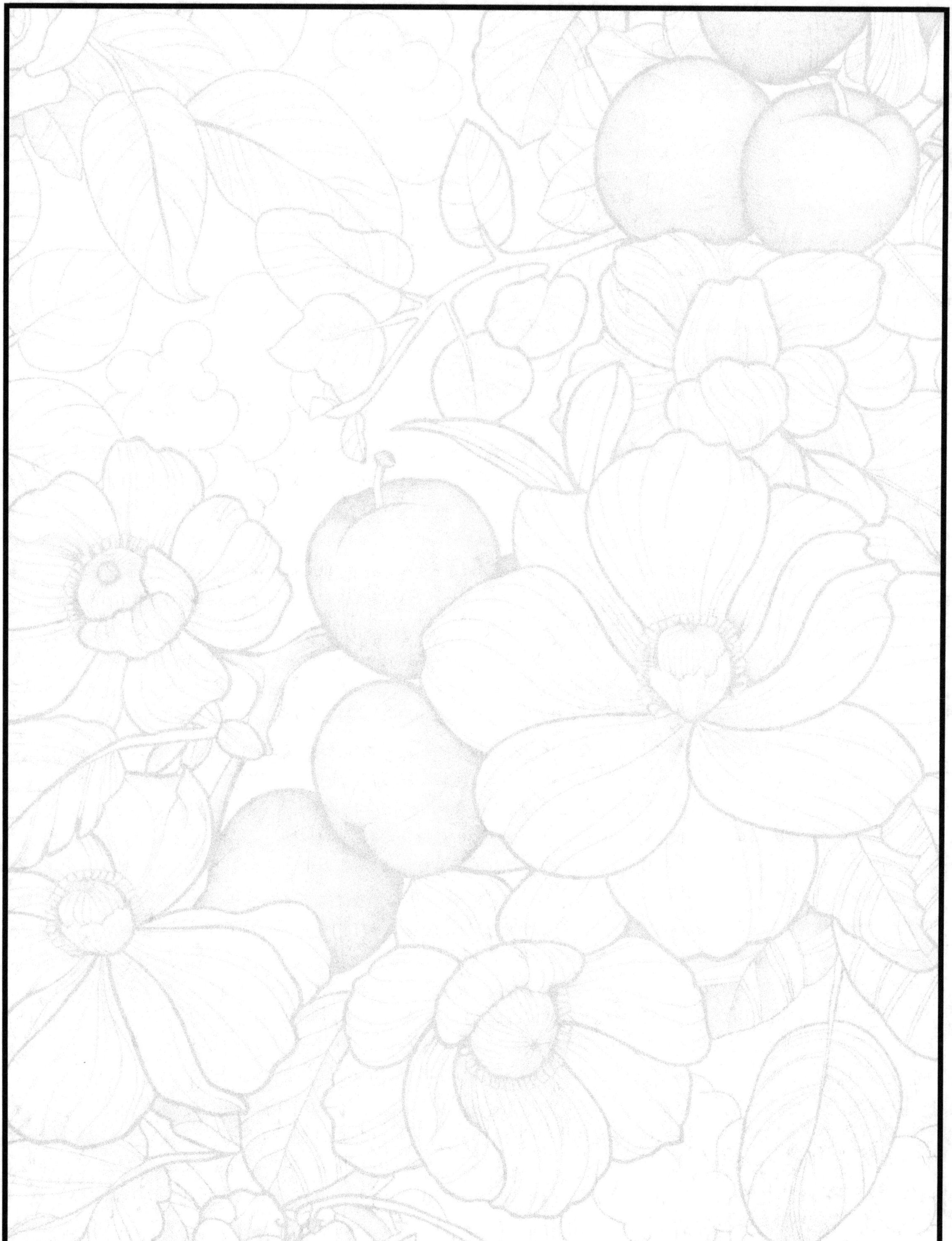

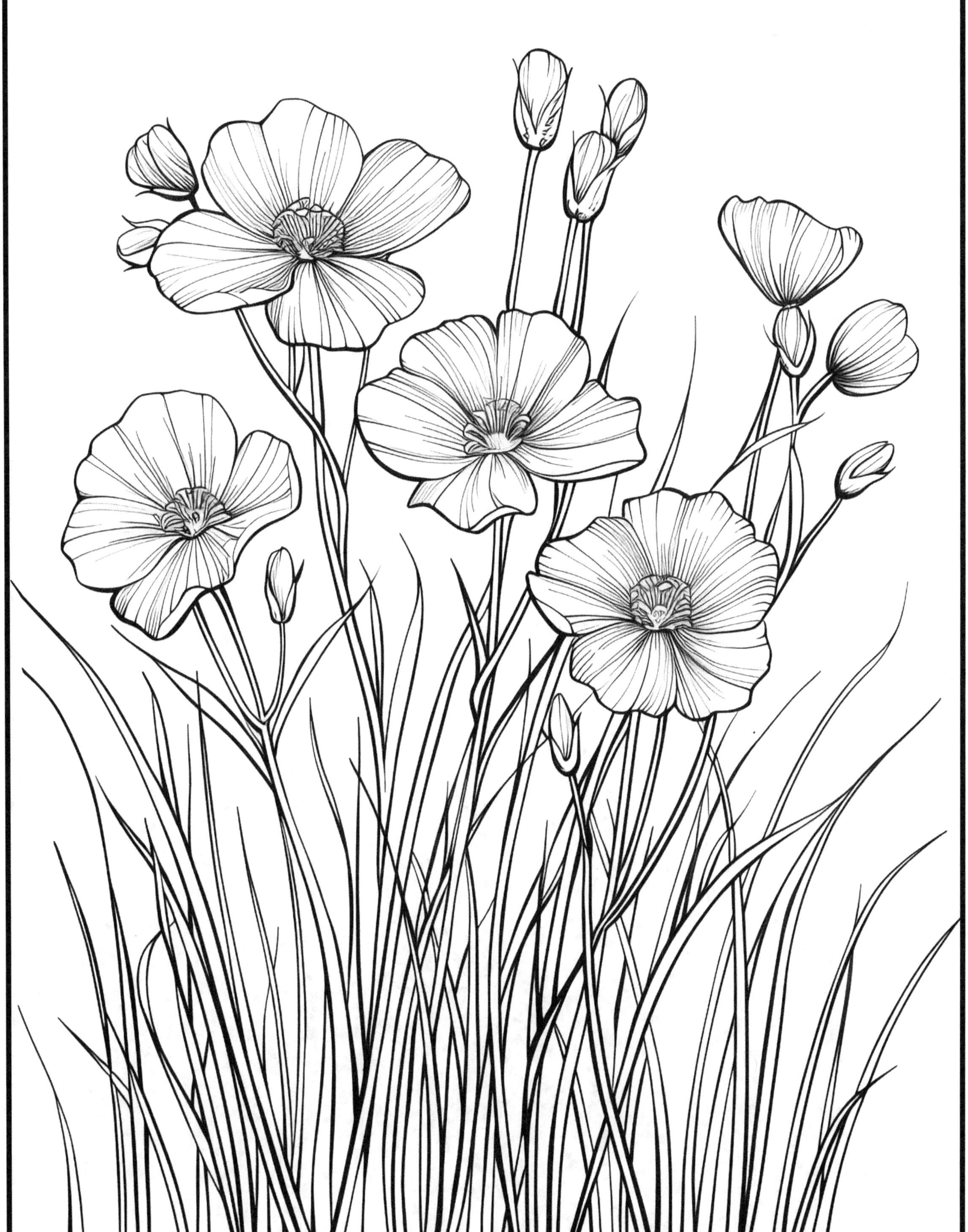

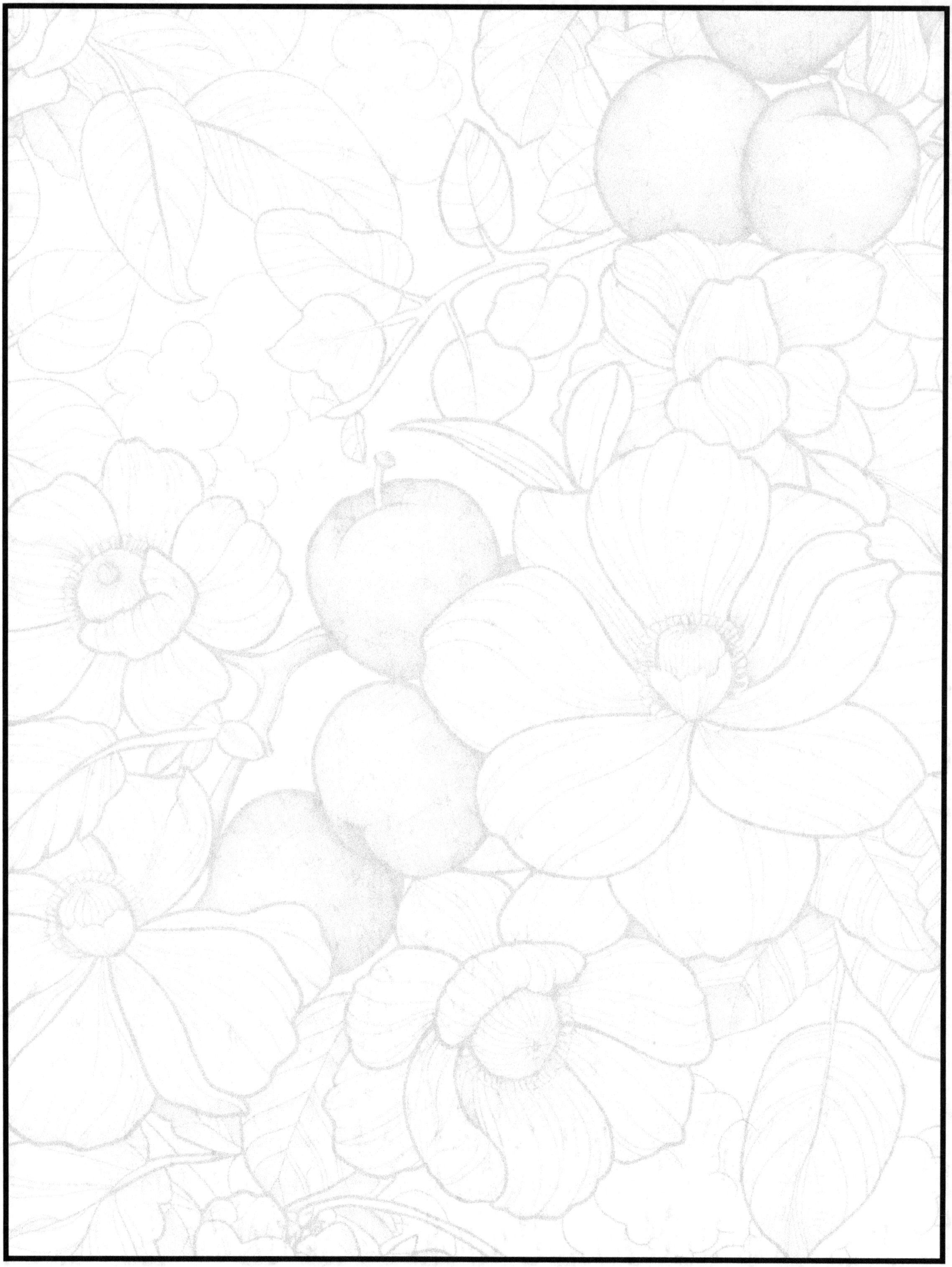

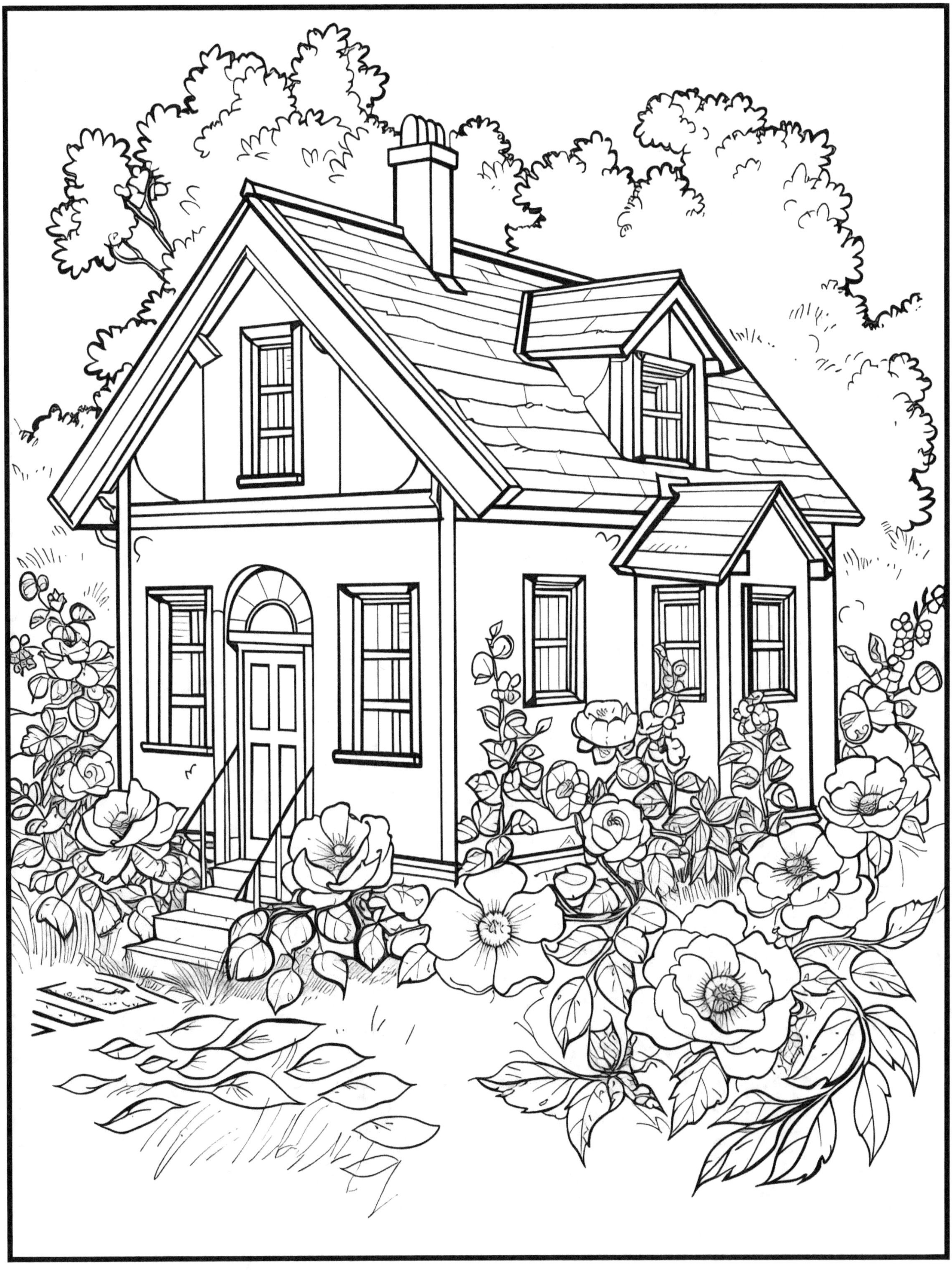

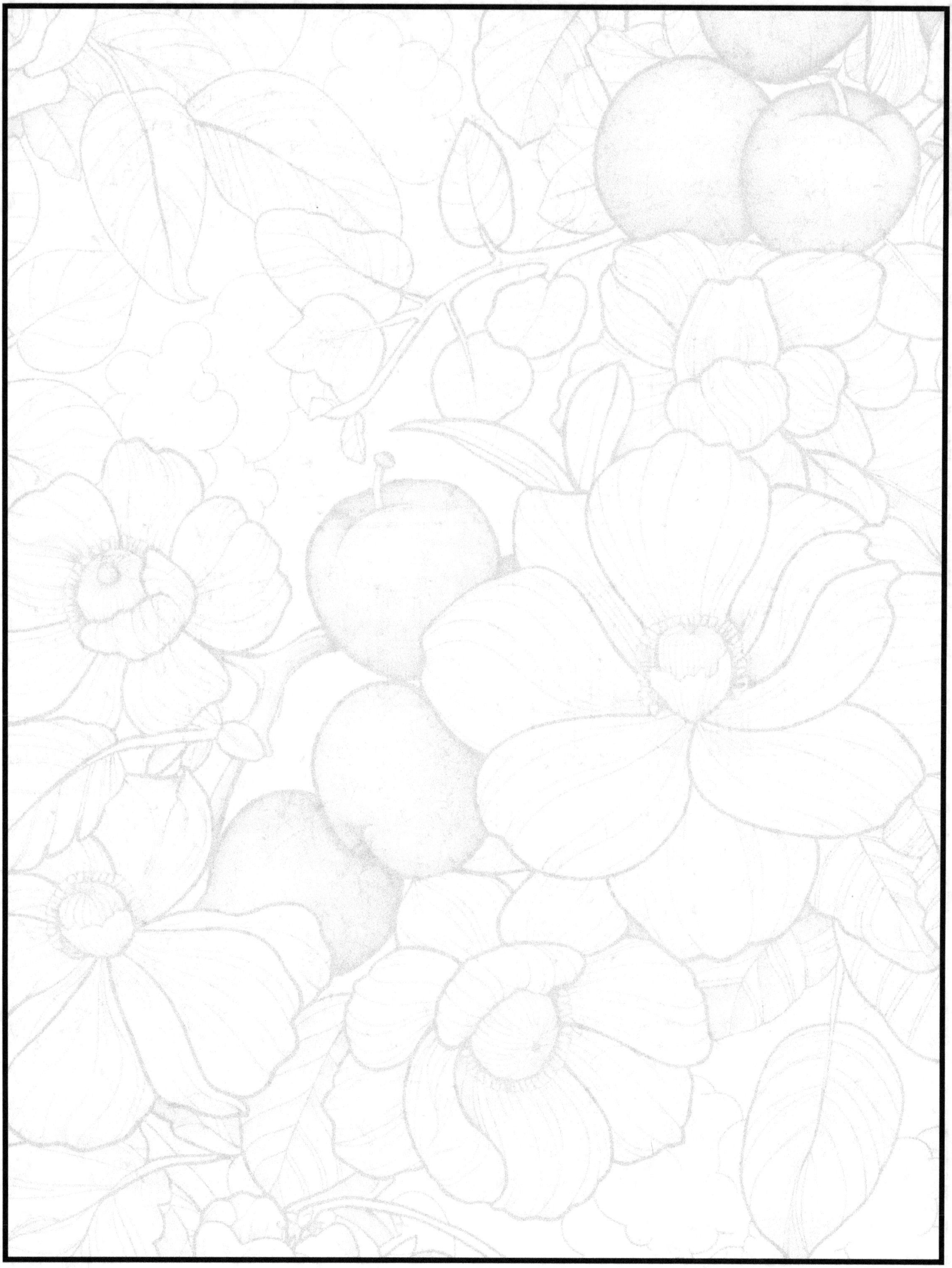

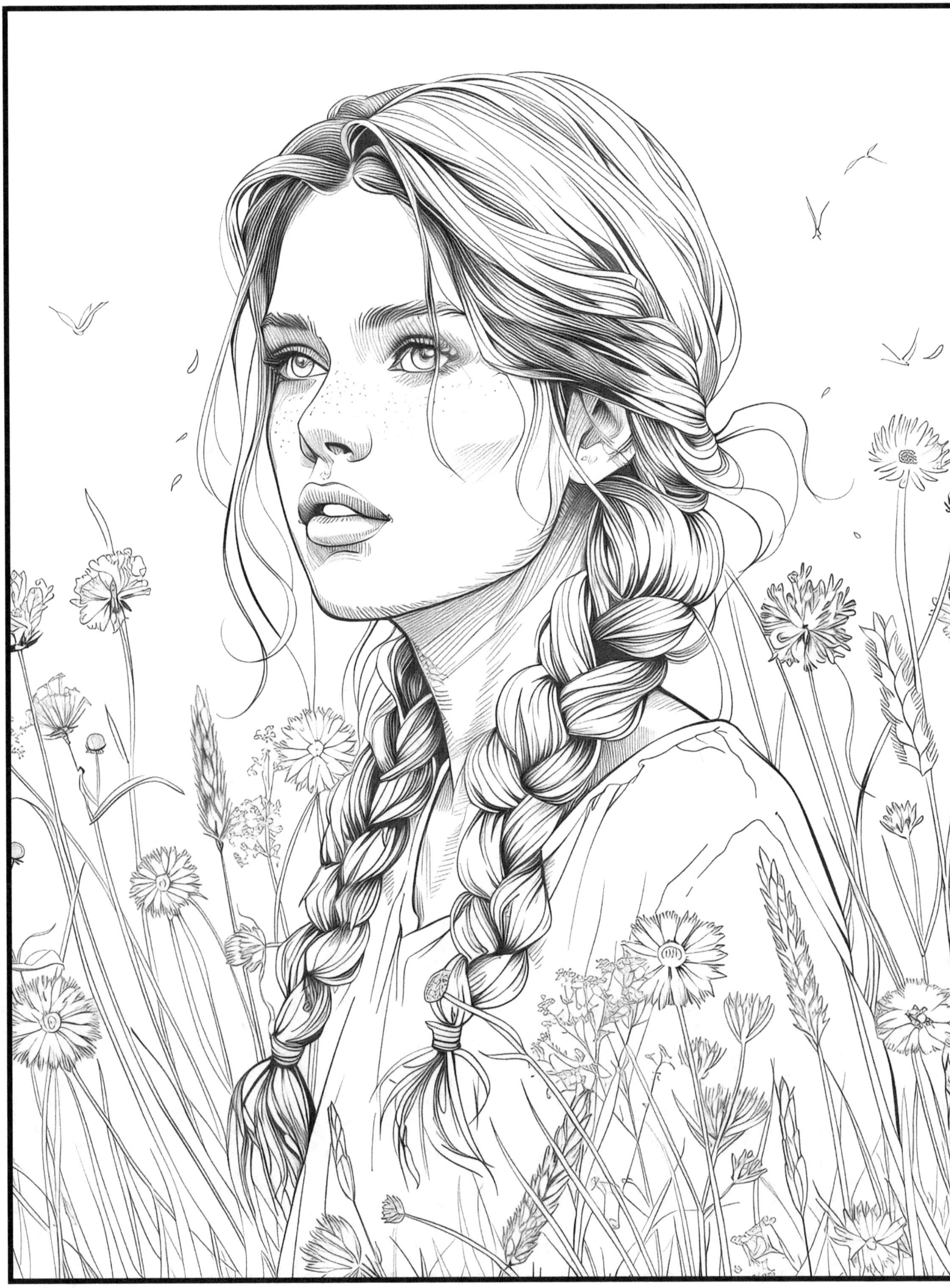

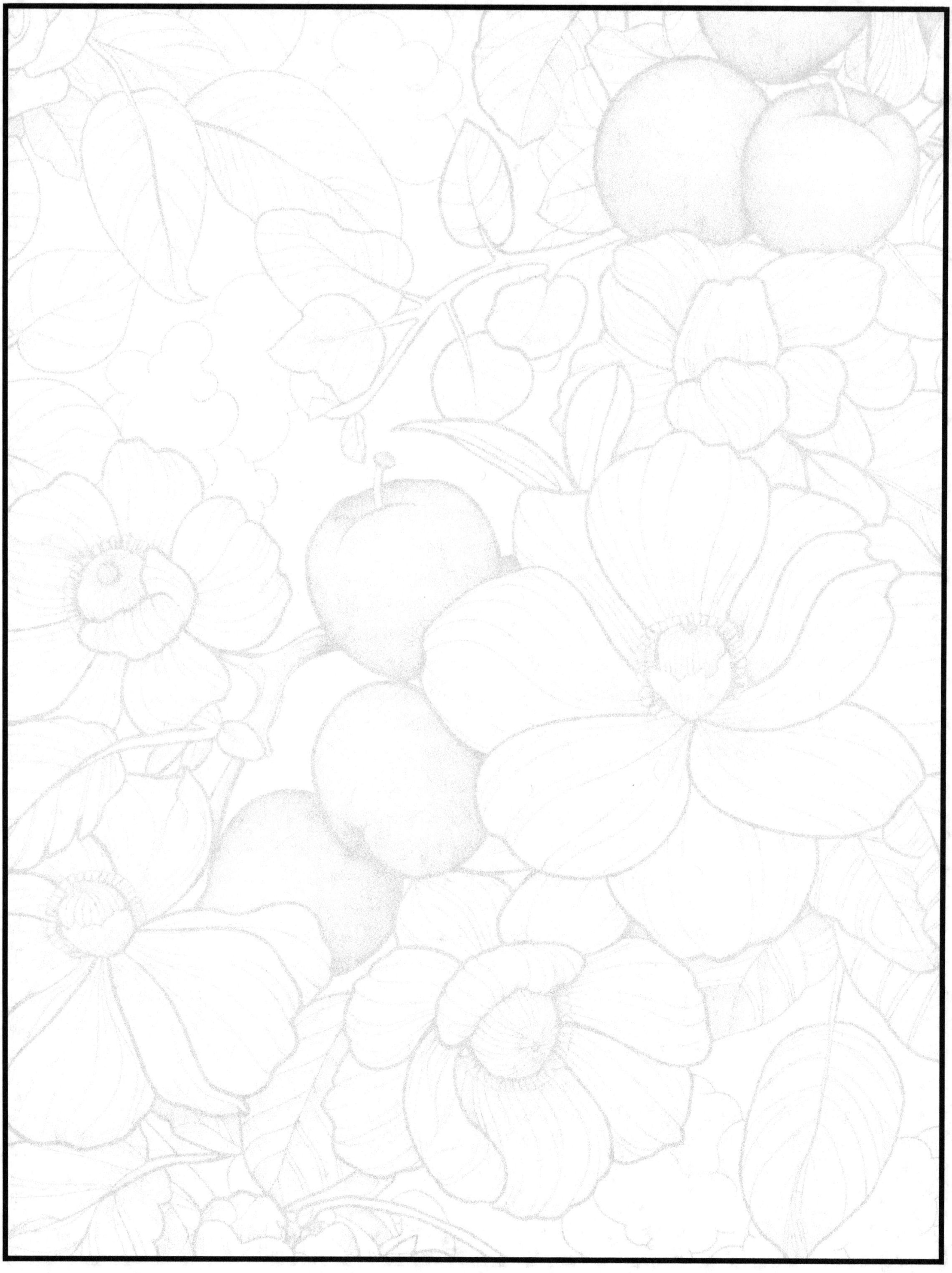

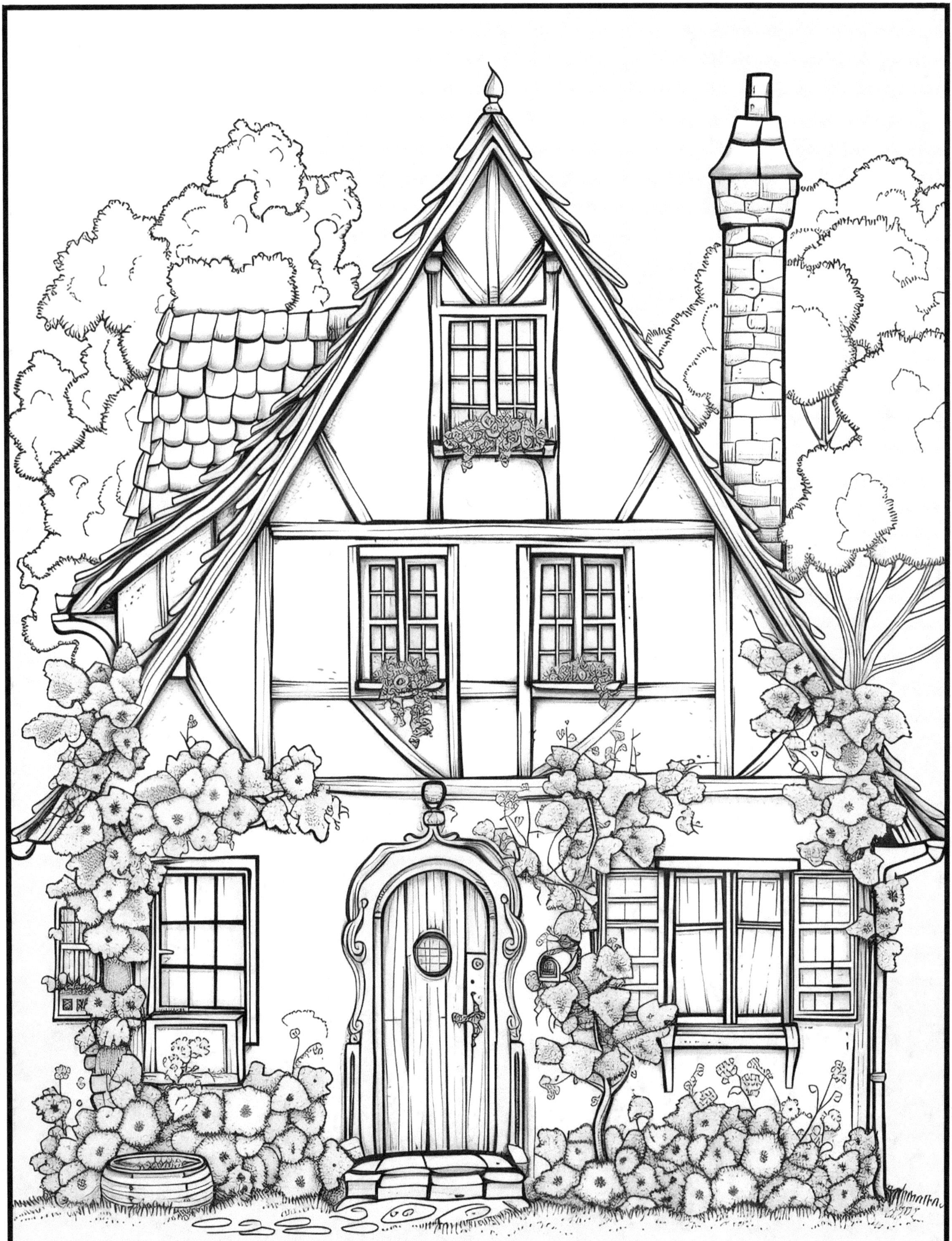

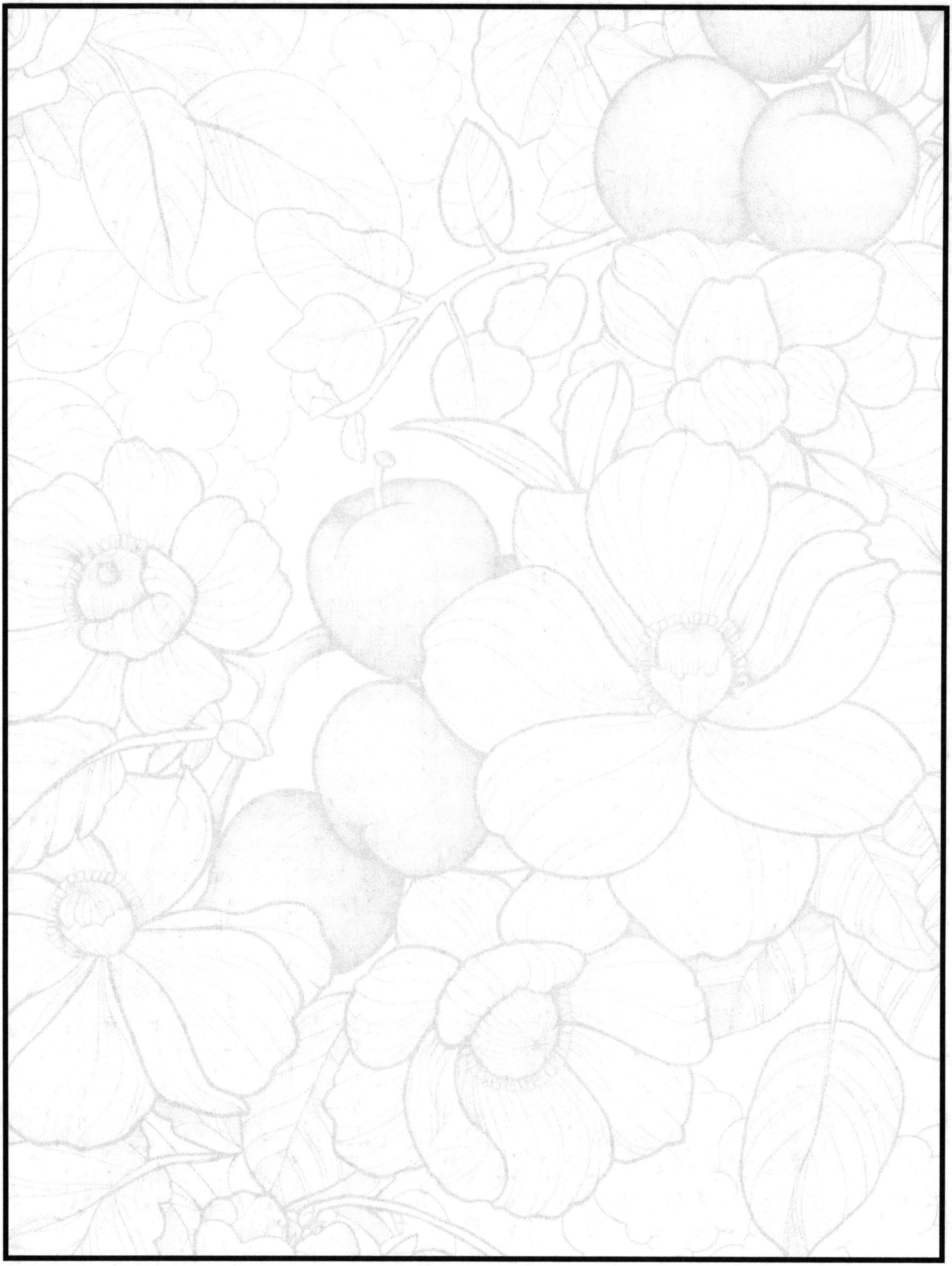

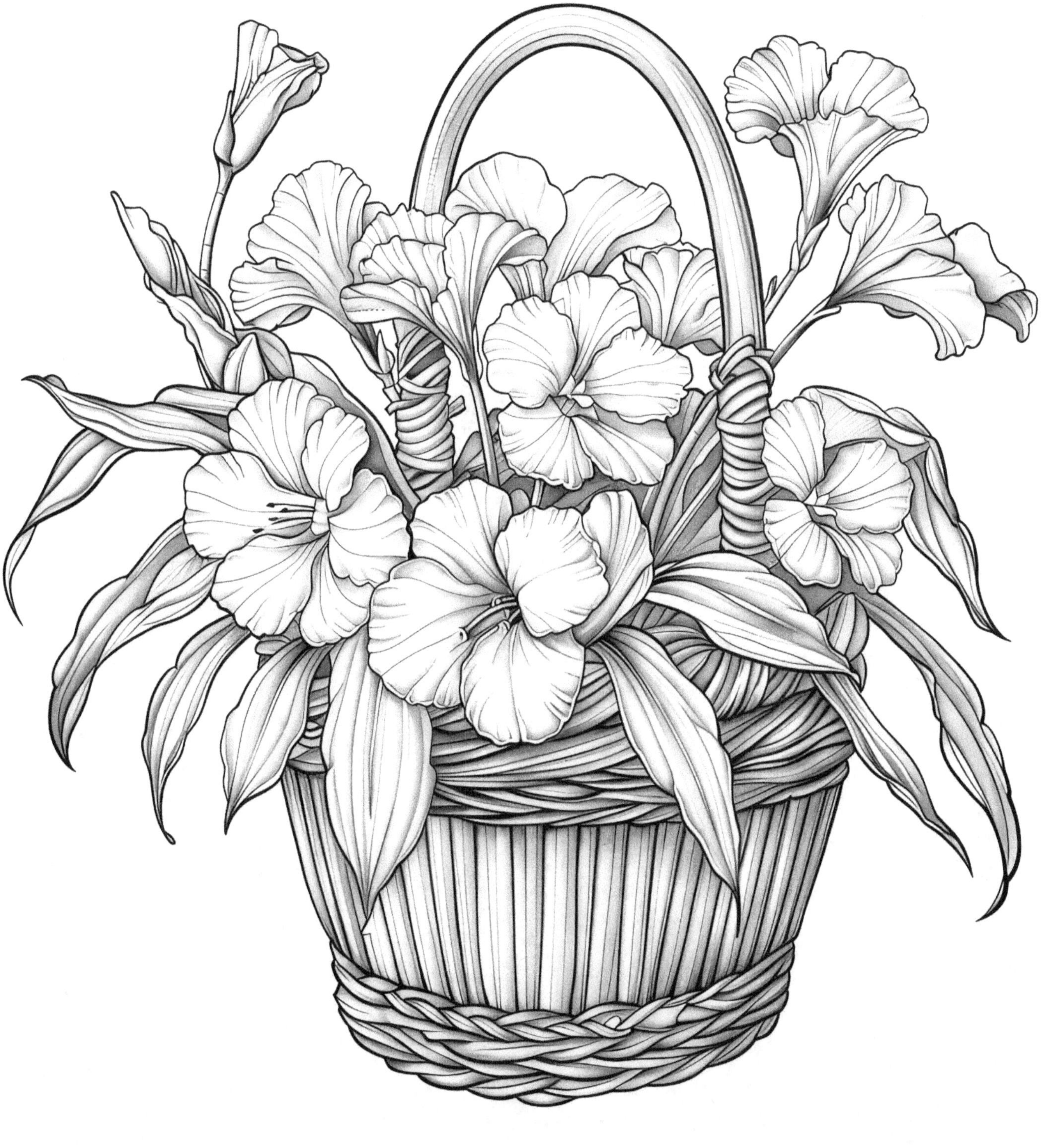

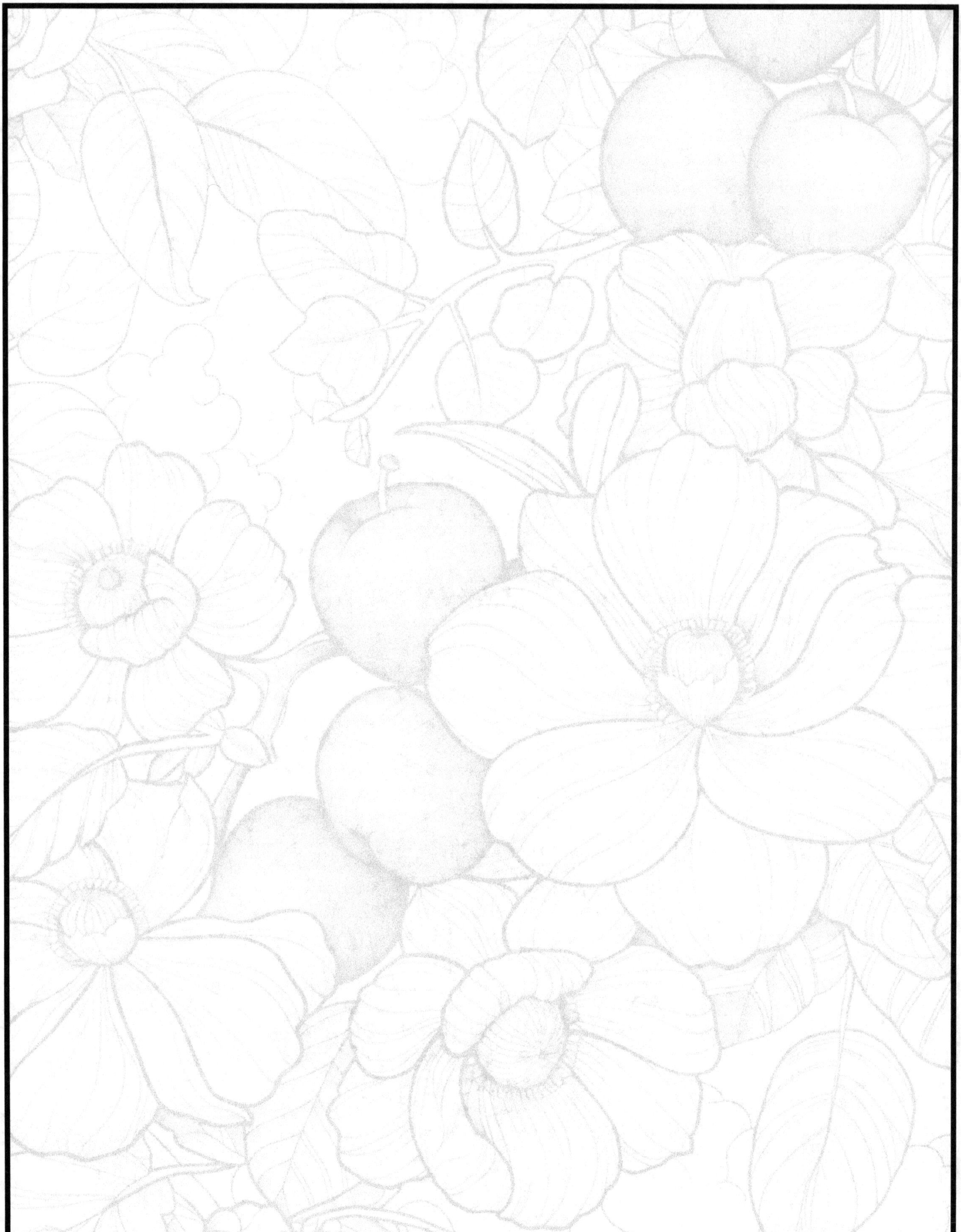

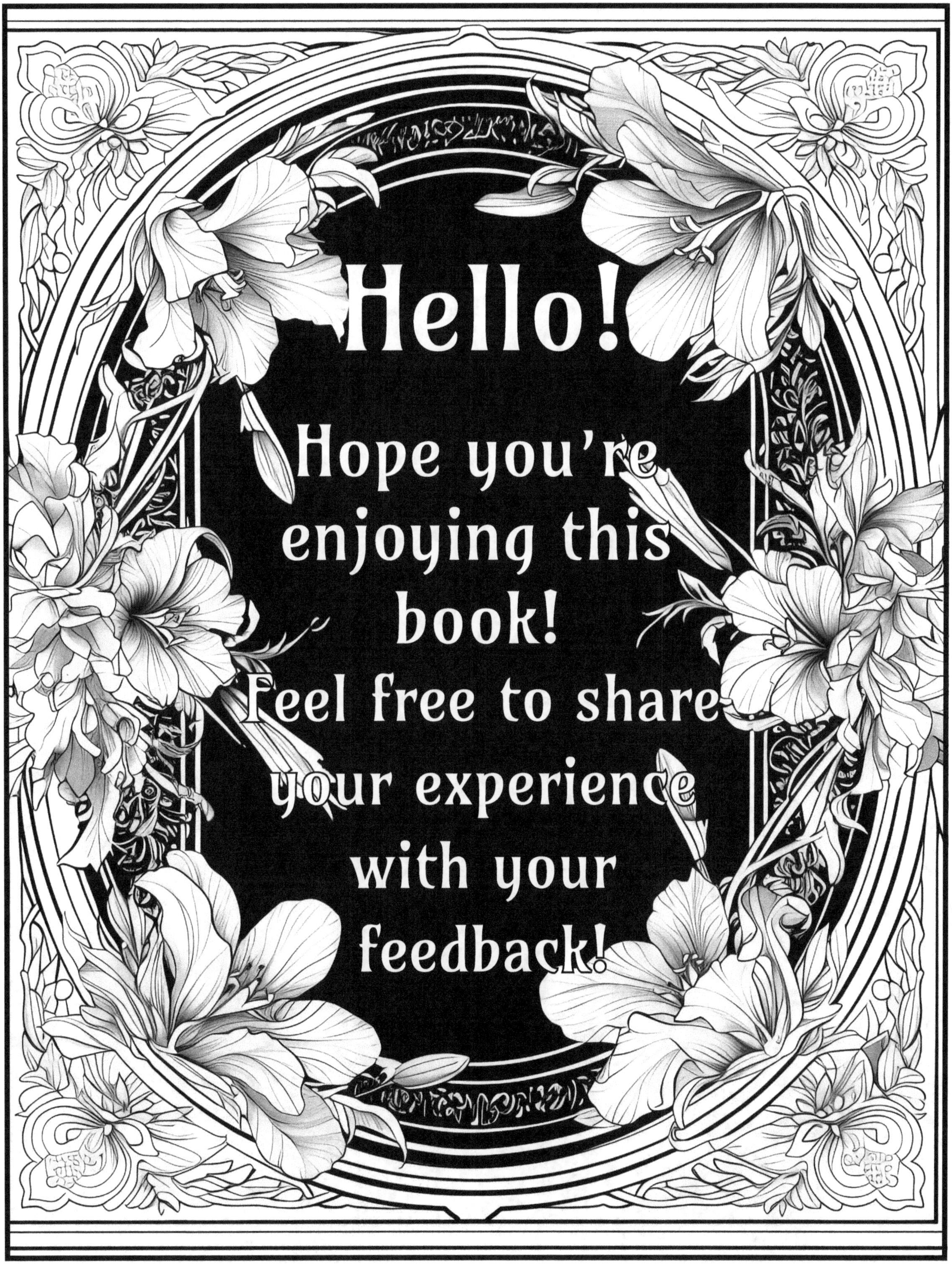
Hello!
Hope you're enjoying this book!
Feel free to share your experience with your feedback!

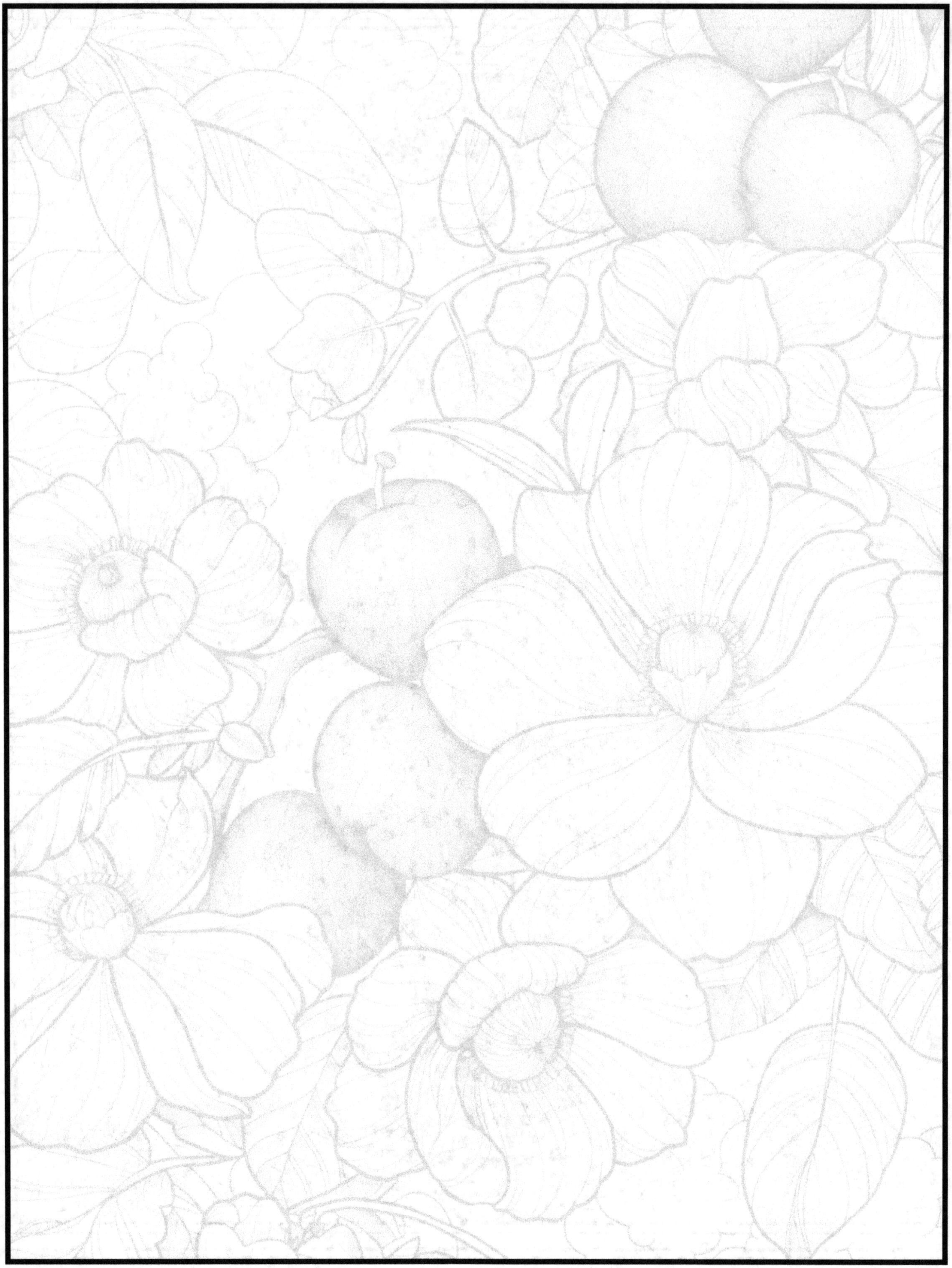

www.ingramcontent.com/pod-product-compliance
Lightning Source LLC
Chambersburg PA
CBHW062122220526
45471CB00010B/3834